PRAISE FOR DARE TO DECIDE

"Anyone could relate to times of feeling stuck as Emily describes them. I love how she weaves her personal story together with practical ways to get started unraveling the chaos in our minds right from the first chapter. I'm excited to see how this book will help people get unstuck and start living their God-sized dreams."

—Brenda Drost, speaker and
founder of brendadrost.com

"In *Dare to Decide*, Emily provides powerful, psychologically sound tools to help you face and move beyond the fears that hold you back. Conversational, honest and actionable, Emily's words will inspire you to get unstuck and start moving towards a life of adventure and fulfilment."

—Steve Abma, psychotherapist

"Dare to Decide offers gentle and compassionate ways for you to shift from overthinking to finding your best next step."

—Kary Oberbrunner, author of *Your Secret Name* and *Elixir Project*

D0940097

DARE *to* DECIDE

DISCOVERING **PEACE**, **CLARITY** AND **COURAGE** AT LIFE'S CROSSROADS

EMILY GRABATIN

AUTHOR ACADEMY elite

Dare to Decide
Discovering Peace, Clarity and Courage at Life's Crossroads

Emily Grabatin

Author Academy Elite

Dare to Decide© 2020 by Emily Grabatin.
All rights reserved.

Printed in the United States of America

Published by Author Academy Elite
PO Box 43, Powell, OH 43035
www.AuthorAcademyElite.com

Library of Congress Control Number: 2020907834

ISBN: 978-1-64746-251-2 (paperback)
ISBN: 978-1-64746-252-9 (hardback)
ISBN: 978-1-64746-253-6 (e-book)

Available in paperback, hardback, e-book, and audiobook.

Cover design by Debbie O'Byrne at JETLAUNCH.
Author photo by Lauren Dam

This book is dedicated to anyone who dared to decide . . .
to believe in yourself,
to take a step towards your dream,
and to believe someone else could do the impossible too.
Because of you, someone's life was changed.
Because of you, someone dared to become who their dream
needed them to be.

TABLE OF CONTENTS

PART 1: THE CROSSROADS

PART 2: THE CALL

PART 3: THE COMPASS

PART 4: THE PREPARATION

PART 5: THE DECISION

Part 6: The Journey

FOREWORD

Decisions, decisions, decisions. You make thousands every day. Most are inconsequential, and a few (the most important ones) can be life-altering. After working with people as an ordained minister for over thirty-five years, and having coached individuals and consulted with organizations for twenty-five of those years, I have found one of the greatest stumbling blocks for people and groups trying to move forward is making a decision, any decision, and risking that decision being wrong. Procrastination will kill you before the wrong decision does.

As I review the decisions in life that have caused me the greatest anguish and wasted the most time, I find that they were generally not the ones that made the biggest impact. Being able to prioritize which decisions will have the greatest impact is an art. This book helps you to creatively sketch your masterpiece.

Getting the most out of your life demands that you utilize a roadmap to chart your course. Being a sailor and a pilot, I have learned that you never sail or fly in uncharted territory.

But isn't that exactly the point? Generally, when making a decision, we have never been there before. Where is the map? How does one proceed? There is not always a set thoroughfare or roadway to easily follow as you move forward. Emily's course-charting is worth the investment.

Emily has been a brilliant point of light in many people's lives. She doesn't lurk in the recesses. Rather, she resides inconspicuously behind the scenes with confidence in who she is, where she is going, and what she has to share. Her writing is not merely a compilation of other authors' research. Rather, she tells her story and lays bare her real feelings as she allows you to peer into her journey. She has in fact created her own roadmap, and it is versatile enough for anyone to use.

If you have had the privilege of working alongside her, you will know she is thorough. She doesn't miss the details. She is always first to support and praise everyone on the team. She is instinctively on the lookout for others, and while some may only look for what lies on the surface, she quickly recognizes those moments when you are in too deep. That is when she intersects her experience and expertise and collides them with your impending decision.

Emily has dared to personally journey the road of decision-making. Now, she has documented the pathway. I have watched her as she's navigated through all the high peaks and low valleys of emotion in life—moments when many would have given up and merged into the darkness of defeat. That is not how her story goes. This book is her life journey. It is Emily at her finest and at her most vulnerable moments, and now she shares this with you. Now you can own your journey as well.

This book is like having a coffee and sitting down with the author to chat about what's really happening. No surface babble, no "How's the weather?" or "What did you think about that Netflix show?" As you read through her personal illustrations, you begin to recognize your own indecisive moments and deeply hidden feelings.

This book is a long hike. You don't run through it or breeze over it. There are milestones meant for each reader, and you don't want to miss them. Proceed with caution.

Emily puts unique slants on life situations. As she states, "Often we are too close to our own story . . . to consider a different perspective." Stop at the end of each chapter to review your perspective.

As you read through this narrative, you'll realize that—just as Emily's path didn't lead to the destination she dreamed of—in a truly fulfilled life, no experience is wasted.

I hope this book challenges you in a fresh and positive way. I trust the Biblical references will speak to you in your moment and cause you to know God is your Father. He wants to share His strength and wisdom with you on a moment-by-moment basis. I bless you on your journey.

—Mark Collins
Coach and consultant

INTRODUCTION
ACCEPTING MY DARE

I slouched in my seat during a weekly team meeting. The presenter that morning used a baseball game analogy to deliver his leadership insights. My innovative, experienced, educated colleagues were into it, but it wasn't my cup of tea. Soon I zoned out, tuning into a much more familiar signal—the nagging feeling of ordinariness and insecurity. The feeling of being the odd one out.

My attention rested on a passionate big dreamer in the room. He lived by his motto, "You were made for greatness," and he genuinely believed it about anyone he met. It inspired hope in me, but I knew I could never do something as significant as he was called to.

I was the admin girl at my church. Hiding behind a computer, I handled registrations, managed projects, and troubleshot databases. It had been my dream job once—safe, satisfying, and meaningful. Though the fast pace and ever-changing ideas kept me focused, I was steady, not energetic. I was reserved, not charismatic. I enjoyed helping the other leaders look good and carrying out their vision, but I had no clue how to have a vision of my own.

Before I knew it, admiration flared into jealousy.

I wished I had a God-sized dream that would help others, but I didn't even know where to start. I didn't know how to think bigger. I wasn't sure I had it in me to do something significant. I didn't have a university degree. I needed tons of alone time to "charge up" enough to be with people. I didn't have special skills or a message to share with the world—I simply liked helping people.

Did I even want the pressure of my own dream? I wanted to believe I was made for more than doing one admin project after another. But . . .

A quiet inner voice interjected my internal ramble.

You're the only one who doesn't believe in yourself. I believe in you. Others in this room believe in you. You're the only one holding yourself back.

I knew the owner of that voice. His opinion meant everything to me. His messages, usually more sensed than heard, came with authority and affirmation. I saw Him as the creator of my purpose, the provider of all I needed, my encouraging companion, my strength.

It wasn't the fact that God was talking to me that caught my attention. It was the startling realization that He was right.

I'd been saying I trusted Him. When I felt overlooked or misunderstood, I went to Him for security and comfort. When life disappointed me, I found my hope and strength in Him. I knew He believed in me and had created me with something special in mind. What was the point of saying I trusted Him if I didn't act like it?

Heat crawled up my neck. The realization felt so loud that I looked around to see if anyone else had noticed.

Had I really been okay with using busyness and comparison as excuses for staying stuck? I had boxed up my dream to write a book and labeled it *irresponsible*. I had settled for hiding behind an excuse: "That kind of greatness is God's will for someone else, not for me."

It would be one thing if it wasn't the right time to dream. But I refused to be the one holding myself back. If I was allowed to become confident, inspiring, and influential, I wanted to figure out how.

It felt like a dare.

So, I accepted the dare that day.

If you asked anyone else, they'd probably say nothing changed about me that day.

I stayed in the shadows because I was still insecure, unsure, and overanalytical. In fact, it was years of the same stuckness before I realized anything shifted for me. It took several more years before I dared to dream uncomfortably and took intentional steps towards my calling.

I forgot about this experience until I made a list of my defining moments. How had I moved from letting life happen to me to figuring out my dreams and taking risks? It did not happen all at once. I saw a pattern in that list. When I leaned into the pain of uncertainty, rejection, and perseverance, I became better for it.

As a young adult I tried to envision a different career or a bigger dream of writing or helping others. But I pictured the person I was then, not who I would be with training and confidence. That insecure, invisible, timid girl didn't have the capacity to dream big or carry it out. First, I needed to increase my capacity.

For some reason, the only vague picture I had was a vision of myself speaking in front of hundreds of people. There was nothing rational about that. When I even dared to speak up in a team meeting of fifteen people, my mind blanked, and my face felt like it was on fire. I didn't feel compelled to be a speaker, nor did I know what I'd even have to say. If I did come up with something to say, writing was more my style. Yet snapshots of myself speaking to groups flipped through my mind's eye like 3D slides in the red ViewMaster I played with as a kid.

What if I really could do something like that one day?

Excitement sparked.

If I was going to stop holding myself back, I couldn't live from my insecurity anymore. And since I still felt insecure, I had to find something bigger than myself to be my motivation. Not knowing what my dream was, I realized I had to start with living by what I knew God saw in me, regardless of how inferior and invisible I felt.

YOUR DARE TO DECIDE CROSSROADS

Part of you feels invisible and inadequate to carry out the size of the vision that's tugging at your soul. What do you do with a dream that's too big for you to handle on your own? You can't help the thought that "ordinary you" has no business impacting a culture or a way of life.

But you want to believe you were made for more. Deep down you know you were made for more than struggling and striving. There's got to be more to life than barely making ends meet in your potential, your relationships, and your spiritual life.

You've been on the fence.

But you've been hanging out at the crossroads of your calling for a while because you're not quite sure where you're going. What path will take you there? How can you make it happen? Who should you listen to along the way?

Like me, maybe a revelation empowered you with enough courage to choose a path and put together a plan—only to land at another crossroads.

Fear clutters your mind.

You find yourself overthinking your crossroads, making you forget who you are, what you truly want, and where you were going. Fresh ideas excite you, inviting more ideas that you don't know what to do with. Overwhelmed by variables and worst-case scenarios, you slip into a drought of inspiration.

Still, something inside you wants to burst out.

It squeezes against the walls of your heart, clamouring for light.

Is it too much to want to love what you do? Could you really have the kinds of relationships you want? Will that notion that's been nudging you for years—to write that book, start that nonprofit, or make that career shift—go away? You've worked your tail off to build something that has taken over your life while your soul, body, and family beg for a change.

But what are you supposed to do about it?

Maybe an interest of yours has turned into a passion. Or maybe a passion has turned to disinterest. Maybe the job that once challenged and fulfilled you now sucks the life out of you. You want to make your mark on the world or open the door to an adventure that makes your heart soar, but how? With your current commitments, how will you have the time, finances, and energy to add this to your plate?

You stuff it down again as you have a hundred times before. After all, you have bills to pay and a family that needs you. And, of course, the house doesn't get cleaned by itself.

There's also that inner bully who has its say.

Who are you to think you could have more? You're supposed to be content.

What makes you think you could pull that off? You don't have credentials or the charisma to inspire people to listen to you.

Nobody wants you. The world doesn't need another one of those. Leave it to the people who do it better than you.

You agree with the bully. What you long for doesn't seem practical, possible or affordable.

Yet, restlessness still whispers, *There's got to be more to life than this.*

This is your "Dare to Decide" crossroads.

I'm well acquainted with this crossroads. Sometimes I've handled it with elegance and wisdom. Other times I've wallowed in a swamp of indecision and self-pity.

How have you navigated your Dare to Decide crossroads in the past? With ease because you knew what you wanted and where you were going? Or with indecision and befuddlement?

You can find plenty of apps and guides to help you handle whatever path you choose. They inspire you to dream big and follow those dreams. They promise you can attract good things in your life, crush your goals, and be a confident, likeable person. These resources are great when you know where you're going. But what if you don't? Or, if you have many ideas, how do you know which one to pursue first? And what if what you're dreaming for your life isn't what's *best* for you in this season? Many resources minimize the magnitude of the crossroads moment.

Another challenge at the crossroads is the people in your life who just don't get it. They think you're a dreamer, but they don't see how hard you've been trying to make it happen. Your friends tell you, "Quit being indecisive!" You defend yourself, saying, "I prefer to stay open," "It's not time yet," and "Things will get better." Your family tells you, "Stop procrastinating and get it done already." All you can say in reply is, "It's complicated."

Everyone seems to sum it up as, "Here's a good option. Make a plan, and now go do it." I've been on that side, too. I even coach people through those journeys.

But it's not that simple. If it was, why would you keep showing up at the same Dare to Decide crossroads with an eerie case of deja vu? What can you do when the crossroads are shrouded in fog and you don't know what you want or even how to *find out* what you want?

I understand what it's like to feel immobilized by the ache—that ache to be more than you are, to achieve something meaningful, or even to just make a wise decision—yet have no clue what to do. It may feel scary walking through the fog, but with each step you'll find clarity.

Friend, you were on my heart when I mapped out this book. You were made for more than the daily grind. More than making ends meet. More than the list of *should's*, *can't's* and *I wish I had's*. It's scary to feel, to be petrified of rejection, tentative from disappointment, and too uncertain to put yourself out there. Yet finding peace, courage, and clarity in your #madeformore path despite fear is possible. Let my belief in you kickstart your journey. Find space for your intuition, desires, and dreams to breath. One small dare at a time, you can walk towards confidence in your direction and strategy.

YOUR PATH WON'T LOOK LIKE MINE

My husband and I once took a DISC personality assessment to prepare for a conference.

When we finished, he glanced at my results summary and did a doubletake at my low "Decisive" score. "What? You can't make a decision?"

I laughed. "You didn't know?"

If you're a more decisive or adventurous person like my husband, this book will either drive you nuts or help you empathize with the cautious people in your life. You barely notice your crossroads because you choose your path and keep moving without second-guessing yourself. Adventure beckons you, and you flourish under pressure. You simplify things in a way that baffles more vigilant decisionmakers. There's not so much of a "right" or "wrong" way to embark upon your path as there are *different* ways. Someone who loves new ideas will experience different challenges than the one with the slow-and-steady approach to life.

> Transformation emerges when the truth you need to embody saturates your heart layer by layer.

Through this book we're going to have meaningful, reflective conversations as I outline my framework to approaching pivots.

I'm going to share stories—not only because I love stories, but because they make concepts come alive. Transformation emerges when the truth you need to embody saturates your heart layer by layer.

WHERE DOES GOD FIT?

As I wrote this book, I grappled with choosing the spiritual lens that would be most helpful. According to one study, eighty percent of North Americans believe in God or a higher power[1], so the issue wasn't whether to include a God perspective. My quandary was how I could be authentic while opening a safe conversation to explore what's important to you. Is it possible to do this without tripping over controversy?

Some of my friends believe in the God of the Bible: One who loves them, talks with them. Because they believe God lovingly created them, they look to Him for their guidance and purpose. Thus, they welcome insight that's saturated with wisdom and stories from the Bible.

I have other friends who believe in God, but even though they love Him and pray to Him, they rarely feel He's responding. Disappointed by their failed expectations of God, of life, or of others, disillusionment colours their view. They respond to references to faith and the Bible with skepticism and pain.

Still other friends have a respectful view of God, yet they don't see how He is relevant to their crossroads.

Whatever camp you're in, I hope you will find the enlightenment you need while I remain transparent about the God-infused experiences and perspectives that have influenced me. How you interpret my experiences is up to you. All I can do is be upfront about my approach so you don't feel as if I sneaked God in or didn't include enough of Him.

WHY YOU'RE FEELING STUCK

When you've been stuck at your crossroads for a while, it most likely has to do with one (or more) of four reasons:

- **Insecurity**—you're held back by fear, low self-esteem, or lack of confidence in yourself, your worth, your abilities, or your experience.

- **Lack of clarity**—you don't know what you don't know; you have an incomplete vision of what you want, of what's possible for you, or how to move forward.

- **Misalignment**—what you believe about yourself, your options, your values, or your approach doesn't line up with how you're designed.

- **Productive waiting**—something inside you needs healing, a foundation needs to be set, or an external situation needs shifting before you are released to run.

If you're like me, it's not enough for someone to identify the problem and design a solution for you. As much as you might *want* it done for you, your greatest wish is for the certainty that you discovered it on your own. To get there, you might realize your next best path is to pay off debt or make a major investment. Maybe the best decision is to wait or to learn, or maybe it's to map a path and make a leap.

Overthinkers tend to mull through all the variables and prolong making a choice. However, a decision unmade is still a decision. It won't go away. Neither will problems or more options. With each decision comes a new situation to navigate—a setback, a surprise, a new understanding or dynamic. With that situation comes a new decision. Instead of staying stuck, avoiding making decisions, what if you found a better way for decision-making?

Friend, you are not a mistake.

Let's paint a picture of what's possible for you so you can give yourself permission to dream and discover your options. Then, let's walk the journey of trusting your choices, mapping your plan, and taking deliberate action that aligns with your identity and values.

I want you to feel the pride and exhilaration of having weighed your options, crafted a wise decision, and stepped out in faith. Imagine the awe of reaching the destination of your dreams—or transforming so much along the way that you find something even better.

You get to dare to decide.

Excited?

Let's do this.

PART I

THE
CROSSROADS

1

CAMPING AT YOUR CROSSROADS:
What Is This Really About?

*"Getting to the next level always requires ending
something, leaving it behind, and moving on. Growth
itself demands that we move on. Without the ability
to end things, people stay stuck, never becoming who
they are meant to be, never accomplishing all that
their talents and abilities should afford them."*

— Henry Cloud, *Necessary Endings*

When I look back at my twenties, I was eager to
serve and hungry to grow and learn, but my world
felt small. I kept it contained because I immersed
myself in one commitment at a time. Back then it was my
work at my church. I was comfortable in the shadows, merely
maintaining my emotional and physical energy. Unfortunately,
those shadows were the perfect place for a victim mindset to
lurk.

To go somewhere intentionally, you have to see your destination and believe you can get there.

Such a simple statement.

Yet your epiphany can come in a swift moment or drag on over years as your soul scraps its way through urgencies, disappointments, and responsibilities.

Externally, crossroads are turning points that announce things will never be the same. They might look like a pregnancy, a health complication, or a job loss. Sometimes we welcome the change. Other times we feel it is a hassle or an interruption to our plans. These are the twists and turns that keep the story of life intentional. Without an event significant enough to catch our attention, life carries on.

We endure jobs, bring our kids here and there, pack our schedules with getting stuff done—then, at the end of the day, wonder what we actually accomplished. When we start getting restless, hating our work, tiring of the constant hustle, we deal with it the only way we know how. We hide through busyness, convinced it's the ticket to fulfillment. We fill our schedule with work, achievements, or volunteering. Then, we numb our heart with novels or Netflix so we can keep going. Actually admitting and committing to our dream might interfere with the people depending on us, so we tell ourselves we'd better not disrupt that.

While a crossroads is an event with external distinctions, internally, crossroads are defining moments that shape who we're becoming. They force us to evaluate our priorities. They are opportunities to rise up, to thrive in your purpose in any circumstance.

Maybe your life was perfect. Everything was on track. Your plans were made. Your marriage was idyllic; you were enjoying life. A hard season started getting more manageable, and you finally figured out your new rhythm.

Then the crossroad appeared.

An end of a path.

A tragedy. A new shift in your family. A loss of a job. A new job. Burnout. A surprise announcement from a family member.

Sometimes the turning point is synced with your readiness. The perfect someone comes along the moment you're ready to start dating again. The new career lines up as your kids start their first week of school. The new business idea emerges during the same week you realize you need a new strategy.

Then there are the crossroads that spiral us into over-thinking, frustration, and analysis paralysis. Our external crossroads—or lack thereof—don't fall in line with our expectations, desires, or needs. God seems silent, and we're stuck in a roundabout of life with no exit.

CROSSROADS REVELATIONS

As I faced the crossroads in my life, I couldn't see the pathway I wanted. The Dare to Decide framework was inspired by where I found myself at my lowest point—the helplessness I had to overcome before I found a new path. As I wrote the first draft of my book, the stories I included felt haphazard and disjointed. If I didn't have a clear, linear path, how would those stories make sense? So, I packed up my laptop and pink sticky notes and headed to my local coffee shop.

Over a couple hours I mapped a timeline of key transitions in my life.

- Getting my first "real" job at eighteen, which filled my savings account

- Embarking on the discipleship program I'd been saving for, then feeling caught in a paradox of awkwardness and fulfillment

- Feeling lost and purposeless at home, which led to immersing myself in an unhealthy sense of purpose

- The night I couldn't stop crying because I couldn't do life without wholehearted purpose anymore

- Moving to a new town

- Getting married

- Landing my dream job

- The day my first husband walked away from our marriage

- The moment I realized I'd found what I was born to do

I had mapped my defining moments before, but I had looked at each one individually to find meaning. This time, as I filled in each year's key moments and noted the significant crossroads, a pattern emerged. Each crossroads didn't stand alone. Together they charted an internal journey of hope.

First, hope led to a peak of delight and exploration. Then, I descended into restlessness and hopelessness. It was in the valley of surrender where the crossroads appeared. Paths of hope emerged when I was willing to accept reality, be brave, and move in a new direction.

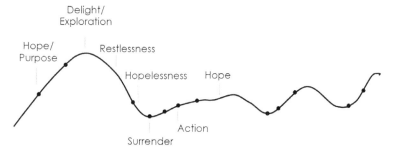

● CROSSROADS DECISIONS

Below/After: Paths of hope emerged when I was willing to accept reality, be brave, and move in a new direction.
Hmm, I thought as I studied the wavy line for a while. Feeling I was onto something, I jotted down what seemed significant about each phase.

Hope and Purpose
- The anticipation of fulfilling experiences and a clear sense of purpose.

- Often accompanied by tangible action toward a goal.

Delight and Exploration
- Experiencing new opportunities

- The bliss of a new adventure, the wonder of seeing things with new eyes, and

- The fulfillment that comes with wholehearted and purposeful living.

- When you choose to keep peace and gratitude in your heart, it's easy to connect daily moments and significant actions to a sense of purpose and fulfillment.

Restlessness
- Eventually the novelty wears off, and you find your-self merely enduring.

- Notions haunt you that something is missing, that you don't quite fit, or that something isn't quite right. Maybe it's because you've changed. Maybe circumstances didn't meet your expectations.

- You hang on to the past and present because it's all you know, and there isn't a clear, open door.

- Life has a sense of drudgery, monotony, and busyness.

- Depression can surface in this stage.

Hopelessness

- Coming to the end of yourself.

- Realizing that things aren't going to be the same or that your desires have changed.

- Your approach to the current reality is no longer working.

- Often accompanied or preluded by a breakdown, burnout, or health problems.

Surrender

- Accepting a new reality, learning a new way of being and doing.

- Often accompanied by rest, retreat.

- Your actions come from a place of trust, releasing the outcome.

- It means being fully, vulnerably you with no mask or sense of needing to earn results.

Action

- With a new mindset come new habits. Building new habits can feel cumbersome or satisfying.

- Sometimes it means trying new things, hanging out with a new circle of people, and establishing new routines.

- Each new action invites a fresh perspective. You see opportunities you may not have been ready for (or recognized) before.

Hope
- Fresh vigor in anticipation of new, fulfilling experiences.

- A clear sense of purpose or divine assignment.

I noticed a couple of things in the peaks, valleys, and in-between spaces spanning twenty years. First, over time the space between each stage shortened. With each crossroads came an opportunity to "upgrade" into a new version of myself. I was relieved to realize that the more self-aware I became, the more my confidence and maturity grew. The sooner I recognized the responsibility within each stage and adopted a growth mindset, the sooner I transitioned into the next stage.

Second, the events themselves weren't the lifechanging crossroads I first expected to see. They only marked the journey I was already on. Sometimes the crossroads came with the stage I was in. Maybe it was divine timing. Perhaps I was ready to recognize an opportunity that had always been there.

Imagine you're in the job you once enjoyed (hope). In your first couple of years you gained skills and made some fascinating connections (delight/exploration), but now it has become tiresome (restlessness). You consider other career paths, but it's too risky for you to make a big shift in your life, so you continue to tough it out (hopelessness). One day you find out your coworkers were laid off. Suddenly you wake up inside and realize your job—and financial security—might not be as stable as you thought it was. It could have been you who was laid off. You even wish it had been you—then you'd be forced to find a new career direction. That's when you realize the truth: now is as good a time as any to look for new options (surrender). With excitement renewed, you begin looking at college degrees and career options (crossroads of hope).

Seeing these life events in a greater context, I realized they were pivot points that changed my direction only when my heart, mind, and soul changed too. I might not always be able to choose the events that happen in my life's story, but I can sure choose what kind of character I want to be. And that changes the entire tale.

WHO IS YOUR DREAM CALLING YOU TO BE?

Most characters in novels don't think ahead about what they'll need to do to get to the climax of their story. They would crawl into a cave if they had even a hint of what they were about to face.

When we're introduced to them, we usually encounter them in their ordinary life. They start out as . . . well, what they are. Kind. Generous. A rescuer trying to solve everyone else's problems. Immature. Preoccupied. Success-driven. Finicky. Maybe they're aware of why they are the way they are, maybe not. Much has shaped the person they are: Little choices they make in response to things that happen. The authority and culture around them. The people around them. Opportunities they've been given. Their expectations of life and how those expectations were fulfilled or unfulfilled. Their attitudes toward life. All the readers know, though, is what we catch from our glimpse of their everyday world.

Then, something happens that launches them into a new story. An ending. An opportunity. An experience or revelation breaks their heart, and the burden won't leave.

Suddenly this victim or bystander starts a hero or heroine's journey. Something that matters more than comfort or uncertainty makes it worth the risks and challenges they're about to face.

This is what your crossroads is about.

Discovering and living the dream in your heart means stepping into who you were meant to be and what you were called to do. This will impact more than your own happiness and fulfillment. It will inspire others to do the same. How might our world change if we dared to do something about it? We'd see depression lifted, better marriages, happier children. People who are enslaved would find freedom and purpose. Insecure women would find confidence.

DO I HAVE WHAT IT TAKES?

When I accepted the dare in my team meeting years ago, I had to face that I didn't have what it takes even to dream a bigger dream, let alone do something different with my life.

Often, when our identity, success, or dream is on the line, crossroads moments make us face where we are now, where we need to be, and what we need to get there. We might not have the discernment, courage, and skills we need to tackle the next stretch of our journey. Crossroads demand more of us than we've ever given before. At some point it seems like our options come down to a choice between quitting or going on.

When we base our options on where and who we are now, we risk missing out on becoming all we're meant to be.

Imagine becoming at peace with yourself. You're confident in who you are and what you have to offer whether in seasons of servitude or revelry. Humble about how far you still have to grow, you're generous because you're firm about your boundaries. You live wholeheartedly in the present: in the best, the dull, and the disconcerting moments.

What if your evolution was like that of an ideal but worthy character you would love to become if you were in a story? That means building character, which psychologist Henry Cloud defines as "having the ability to meet the demands of reality.²"

Changing the question you ask yourself can give you the perspective you need to move forward. Asking, "What if I don't have what it takes?" won't get you far. This question, though, might help: "If the resources I counted on before (knowledge, relationships, courage, tools, skills, systems, strategies) won't cut it for the next phase of the journey, what do I need to do to develop them further?"

Knowing who you are and who you can become impacts how you view your options for the future.

Dare to be Honest with Yourself

What are your crossroads?
What is making you feel stuck?
How long have you felt this way?

2

FINDING YOURSELF STARTS
WITH LOSING YOURSELF

"I'm not lost for I know where I am.
But however, where I am may be lost."

— Winnie the Pooh

I was twenty the year I lost my purpose—two years after living my dream.

When I was fourteen, I started noticing the monthly newsletters my parents received from Mercy Ships, a nonprofit organization that sent hospital ships to third world countries[3]. I would linger over stories of the hope and transformation the volunteer medical team and crew brought to those they served. Pictures of head-sized tumors, babies with cleft palates, and post-surgery smiles captivated me. Professionals were giving up weeks and years of their lives to perform operations and offer community development training. Others joined the crew to serve by housekeeping or managing the cafeteria. I wanted to be a part of that!

I had no desire or vision to be one of the doctors, nurses, or professionals. Serving those who were there to do the frontline work sounded fulfilling enough for me.

For three years I stashed away the money I earned. After graduating, working for a year, and getting an online administration diploma, it was time. I applied for a five-month discipleship school on one of the ships. This program would help me understand the Bible more and offer practical ways to serve the needs of a third world country. Hungry to learn and to experience adventure, this seemed like an ideal way for me to share my love for Jesus.

This organization's culture was big on faith. I had heard stories about people who would serve for a few months, intending to go back to their normal life. At the end of their term, they'd feel a sense, a calling to stay for another two years. Often it was the worst thing in the world for them. They fought the call and tried to argue with God, digging in their heels before reluctantly giving in.

I secretly hoped that would happen to me.

I wanted something different for my life. What was the point of simply picking a career path, waiting to meet someone to marry, and living a "normal" life?

In July 1997 I left for Duluth, Minnesota where the *Caribbean Mercy*[4], the South American medical ship, was docked for a PR tour. I devoured the discipleship training. Because it was classified as a crew ship, we had to train for ship crew basic training, so I plunged into frigid Lake Superior and ran around obstacles in a fire suit. We each had designated ship chores, and mine was dishwashing. It came with clear expectations, a beginning and an end, and a skill I could master. And that excited me. During mealtimes international staff members intrigued me with stories of their experiences on the ship.

While Princess Diana's funeral played on every TV in the nation, I was cataloging donated eyeglasses. I loved that part of the project. What was unforgettable was the tearful "wow" smile of a woman at the pop-up clinic in Guatemala a few months later. She came in to have her eyes examined, and I helped her find eyeglasses that matched her prescription. Hers was the same "wow" grin I'd had at age seven when I put on my first pair of glasses and saw blades of grass in the lawn and leaves on trees instead of a blur.

Yet, living my dream wasn't all bliss.

Much of the time I felt awkward and homesick. As an introverted homebody, I was content to spend hours alone, writing, walking in woods, or disappearing into novels at home. On the ship I was always surrounded by people. When they were ready to have fun, I craved solitude. When I wanted to connect, I lacked the self-confidence to invite myself into their circles.

After five months of new experiences, friendships, and perspective, the final week approached. The other twenty-two students chatted about their plans. Some had decided to stay on the ship—just like the stories I had heard. Others planned to go back to university, get married, or figure out a new relationship.

But I had no clue.

I was getting desperate to know my purpose and direction.

I felt lost. If God created me, wasn't it His job to show me my purpose? One wrong choice and it could change the trajectory of my life. And if it wasn't significant, what was the point of life? I begged God to call me to stay on the ship longer. Figuring out the financial support part sounded like hell, but I figured if He called me, He would provide.

Finally, I hunkered down in my bunk with my journal and Bible and told God, "I'm not budging until I know what You want from me."

In my stubborn stillness, the words came. *Go home. I want you to stay in Canada and impact your own generation.*

My heart sank. Well, *that* sucked.

15

"What does that even mean, God? Can you get a little more specific? What the heck am I supposed to do with that?" Silence.

So, I returned home, feeling more lost than ever. Everyone in my hometown was continuing with their lives. I didn't know a soul in the young adults' group at church. I had just experienced something lifechanging, and I wished I had someone who could help me process everything. Instead, all I had was a calling I didn't understand.

Broke, I resumed working at my previous job to restock my savings. That was the easy decision. Figuring out what to do with the rest of my life was the daunting question. I knew I wanted to do another course with the same organization, and the thought of learning biblical counselling in Australia made my heart leap. But it was going to take another year or so before I'd have enough money to apply. What could I do with myself in the meantime?

My lack of vision and the feeling of being misplaced nudged me into a friendship with someone who also seemed to feel like the odd one out.

I gravitated to the people on the sidelines, and this girl's dark secrets and emotional baggage gave me a sense of purpose. I didn't know where I fit anymore, so I became everything she needed me to be and spent every spare moment with her. It was easier to pay attention to her pain than to figure out my own feelings. Not only was I working full-time, I had also been trained in Applied Behaviour Analysis and hired to work with a couple kids on the autism spectrum. I found the work fascinating, but two hours of therapy took as much energy as eight hours in my other job. Soon, my few remaining lifegiving friendships grew distant. Activities I once loved, such as singing in the choir, reading, and writing, faded away. Still mad at God for not being more specific about my direction, I distracted myself from misery with small, defiant choices until I became a hollow shell, void of identity, purpose, and joy.

I didn't even realize how empty I was until the night I came home from work and started heaving unstoppable sobs for no apparent reason.

I needed space to figure out my life.

Little did I realize I'd soon be given more space than I asked for. Within weeks of handing in a resignation letter to my employer, my friend and I received an eviction notice from my landlords so their brother could rent the basement apartment instead. A couple days later, mail I had been eagerly awaiting arrived. When I opened it, all I could do was laugh. The letter told me I hadn't been accepted into the school I had applied to.

There's no way this is a coincidence. God, what are you up to?

My life became a blank slate, and I had no idea what to write on it.

Dare to Be Hopeless

The moment you lose hope can be lifechanging. Often, we keep pushing forward towards change, even when it's futile. Realizing the old path isn't what you thought it was going to be can be empowering. In what ways has the path you've been on become hopeless?

3

WRESTLING TOWARD SURRENDER:
When Giving in Is Not Giving Up

"I have wrestled and I have trembled toward surrender."[5]

—*As You Find Me,* Joel Houston, Matt Crocker
& Benjamin Hastings, Hillsong United

Melanie watched the plastic stick she had just peed on, willing the two pink lines to appear. But, like every other time in the past ten years, only one emerged. The lone pink line sat there, oblivious to the disappointment, anger, and pain churning inside of her. She had everything to be grateful for—the love of her life, a job she loved, a beautiful home. Yet this one dream remained: to have a child. After spending her time and savings on tests and fertility treatments, she had arrived at the crossroads. Should they keep trying and praying? Or explore paths of adoption and surrender to more of the waiting game?

In other situations in Melanie's life, surrender was the only way she had found to go on. In her career she had to surrender her desire for a well-plotted path, embracing the unknown. She grew and developed new skills because of it. In marriage she had to surrender the fairytale dream of romanticized love to accept the everyday reality of loving someone imperfect. She surrendered her life-should-be-this-way stress to receive grace. Now, realization dawned that maybe God had a different dream for her, and the only way she knew how to find deep peace and happiness was through surrender.

When we have something we hold dearly—our dream, our identity, our plans—it feels like we need to power through, be strong, and make it happen. But what about when we find ourselves floundering in indecision? It's easy to feel weak and let down.

I confess there are times when I know surrender is my only option, but I don't want to do it. God wants a part of my heart I don't want to let go, but I still want to have a say in the outcome. Secretly I try shortcuts, as if I can somehow fool God. I may even go through the motions of surrender, but deep inside I still haven't let go. Maybe I give up and pout. Or I try to leverage surrender, like pressing one end of a lever to do the heavy lifting on the other end.

Surrender can feel like different things.

Sometimes it feels like a rescue—being pulled out of a situation and into God's warmth and grace.

It might feel like mercy—receiving something you didn't deserve with no way to earn it yourself.

It might feel like stillness—with the courage to be present in your grief, pain, boredom, fear, and the gratitude and contentment that arise in the quietness.

It might feel like acceptance—that your best isn't quite good enough, and that's okay.

It might feel like doing all you know to do while releasing the outcome.

It might feel like powerlessness—admitting you don't have the control you thought you did.

It might feel like faith—trusting there's something you can count on, even though you can't see it yet.

Surrender is not giving up, checking out, or settling for mediocrity.

> Surrender is not giving up, checking out, settling for mediocrity or namelessness.

We are responsible for our part in our crossroads, but the weight isn't all on us. Without connecting to a source greater than ourselves, all our striving and waiting, our success and failures, will feel empty.

The idea that there's power in surrender isn't anything new. Alcoholics' first steps to overcoming addiction are acknowledging they're powerless and submitting to a higher power. Every religion has their version of spiritual surrender. The other day I even came across a book that teaches avid Star Wars fans the practice of surrendering to the Force.

For surrender to have fruitful power, the one you're surrendering to must have a better solution to your problems than you do. I guess the question is, to whom or what are you surrendering?

If I'm going to trust in someone more powerful than me, I'm going to choose the One I believe created me and this beautiful earth. The One who has my best interest in mind. The One who has an abundance of everything we could ask for or imagine. The One who gives good gifts and makes something good in us from our mistakes and our tragedies.

SHAME, SURRENDER, GRACE

A stack of CDs, a notebook, and my Bible sat next to me on the brown carpet of the living room of a friend's home where

I stayed after the eviction. Soulful worship music pumped through the speakers. I had the house to myself for the next few hours, and I let the music wash over me. I realized it had been months, maybe even a year, since I had played the music I loved instead of the music someone else enjoyed. Judging by the date of the last entry in my journal, it had been months since I had been honest enough with myself to see my thoughts in ink.

I knew why.

Facing my shame, disappointment, and inner ugliness wasn't fun. Somehow, I knew I couldn't move past that moment without facing the turmoil within, so that day I made an appointment with surrender.

"Here I am, Lord," I said, my voice cracking.

It felt vulnerable, stepping out from the shards of my brokenness. I had messed up. I was lost, and I was powerless to find my own way back. It's one thing to know someone already knows what you've done. But it takes a lot of vulnerability to stand exposed without excuses, masks, or numbness.

When you run out of words after explaining what you feel, it takes humble courage to be still. The air grows heavy with what's unsaid.

Unable to stand it, I flipped open my Bible. Afraid of what God might say to my heart, it felt safer to read words already written. The pages fell to the book of Isaiah, the part of the Bible most people avoid because it's where God seems to come undone. He'd just spent a few centuries showing a nation that life's a lot better when they depend on Him. He watches these Israelites self-destruct from their selfish, superstitious, and downright evil choices. He speaks to this group of people through some unlucky guys chosen to be prophets. To deliver God's messages of love and His warnings, they do and say some bizarre things to get everyone's attention.

I figured I deserved a rant from God on how much I had gone astray. After all, if it weren't for Him, I wouldn't have lived my dream and gone to a school to learn and deepen my love for Him. Just because I hadn't understood what He tried to show me, I did my own thing—like the Israelites.

My eyes fell on a paragraph in the fourth chapter. Beyond the cultural nuances and references to the grander story God had planned from the beginning, this message flooded my heart:

> *A beautiful future is ahead—you will not always feel this shame. You not only have forgiveness; you will be fully healed. You are noticed, and you count. And you are not alone. God is still with you, someone who will light your way and shelter you whenever you need it.*

As someone who felt invisible, undeserving, and ashamed, this meant everything to me. The moment affected me so deeply that I marked the date beside that passage in my Bible.

When you accept the hand extended to you, your deepest desires can be fulfilled. There's an alternative to feeling undeserving, dirty, or empty. It comes through accepting forgiveness and forgiving—through receiving grace and extending it. Crossroads have a way of magnifying feelings of loneliness and inadequacies. When your next path only comes one step at a time, God offers something more valuable than answers. He offers His presence. In trust and surrender you'll find transcendent peace. You'll know that no matter what, you're going to be okay.

When in His presence you're filled with love, grace, forgiveness, security, comfort, and peace. This not only strengthens your confidence, but it also shapes how you see situations and possibilities.

Dare to Surrender

What does surrender mean to you or look like in your situation?

4

BEGINNING YOUR STORY:
Who Does Your Dream
Need You to Be?

*"The point of a story is never about the ending,
remember. It's about your character getting
molded in the hard work of the middle."*

—Donald Miller, *Million Miles in a Thousand Years*

I magine you've reached the end of your life.

Kids gather around your easy chair and ask you to tell your life story. What kind of story do you tell?

Is it filled with adventures and comic relief?

Is it a series of unfortunate events you'd rather gloss over to spare them the horror?

Is it a series of life lessons showcasing everything you've built?

Is it full of foreshadowing to the day your life really began?

Would you tell a few scenes of your story over and over because they're the only ones interesting enough to share?

Do you embellish details to hold their attention, or would the real story keep them riveted until dinner?

My passion for stories started with reading Enid Blyton adventures and *The Baby-Sitters Club* as a child. This passion carried into my teens as I spent many afternoons plotting and writing novels about girls who were figuring out friendship and life. They discovered hidden caves and waterfalls, faced their family secrets, and found love. As I emerged into adulthood, I found it challenging to reconcile my responsibilities and disillusionment with an imaginary world. Every few years I would pull out a story and rework it with another layer of insight or writing skills.

There's a reason those stories are yellowing in a box in my basement. They're full of naive cardboard characters who were different variations of myself. Life happened to them, and they reacted. When trouble arose, everything resolved blissfully, and they remained unchanged.

The more serious I became about writing, the more I realized my characters and plots lacked the kind of zest that makes you forget to eat or sleep. Curious, I spent hours and hours researching what made my favourite novels so much better than my own writing.

I discovered there's more to a story than exciting events, unexpected turns, and character interaction. A story is much more than stuff happening to people.

For years I thought I didn't have an interesting story because I didn't have many exciting things happen to me. I would shrug away the dull moments and cringe at the naivety. I tried to shove the shameful, regrettable moments into a dark corner of my memory in hopes I could forget them. Mostly I would compare my story to someone else's, and I would prefer theirs to mine.

Sometimes you can choose the events in your story. You can stay on the couch and binge watch your favourite shows. Or you can find a hobby to express who you are. Or you can volunteer and bring hope to someone. When Saturday comes, you can choose whether you go to that wedding, clean the house, or go for a hike.

Then there are the events that make you feel powerless. Someone else's choice to drink and drive that ends a family member's life. Job loss. Divorce. We can't choose our tragedies. We're simply left to pick up the pieces and figure out how to move on.

We're okay with these events in other people's stories. They move us to compassion, selflessness, and justice. Movies would be boring without mishaps or tragedy.

But a compelling plot is more than positive and negative events. So, what is a story? And what makes one worthy of our time and attention?

Bestselling author and master storyteller Donald Miller summarized it like this: ". . . a character who wants something and overcomes conflict to get it."[6]

A story begins with a character.

Your story begins with you—knowing who you are.

Characters were my favourite part of writing stories. I would compile character sketches to track who had what eye colour, personality, special skills, backstories, motives, family members, strengths, and weaknesses.

Put them in different situations, and I would know how each one would respond. Writing about others' lives took the pressure off mine. It helped me work out the complexity of my desires and hang-ups when I wasn't sure what I felt or wanted.

When we're caught in comparison or self-doubt, why is it so hard to be okay with who we are?

LEADING LADY OR BEST FRIEND?

I love how a scene in the movie *The Holiday*[7] shows this necessary awakening. Cameron Diaz and Kate Winslet play characters who exchange homes to escape their stressful, hurting lives for a couple of weeks. While in Los Angeles, Winslet's character, Iris, goes for dinner with a silver-haired, retired filmmaker named Arthur, who fascinates her with his stories of the old days in Hollywood. Halfway through the meal the elderly man blurts out the question that's been bothering him. Why in the world has she come halfway around the world only to spend the evening with an old guy like him?

Iris confesses she's recovering from a huge shock: the guy she'd been in love with got engaged. The retired filmmaker comments that the ex-boyfriend must have been a contemptible fool and notices Iris's surprise at his nailing the guy's character. Arthur tells her it was pretty obvious since the guy let her go. Referring to the films they had just been talking about, he points out the difference between the leading women and the sidekicks. "You are a leading lady," he says. "For some reason you are acting like the best friend."

Iris is flabbergasted. After all her years of therapy, somehow Arthur's simple declaration illuminates the truth she's been needing all along. Of course she's supposed to be the leading lady of her own story.

If Iris had stayed codependent in her emotional mess and went back to her schmucky ex-boyfriend, I would have been disappointed—even disdainful. Sure, I want to identify with someone who has weakness and struggles. But I also want them to step into the best version of themselves and be the lead in their own story. Every time I watch the scene where she gathers her gumption and throws her ex-boyfriend out of the house, I get a little thrill.

A good story invites us into another world. We identify with the characters and experience what they're experiencing. I feel understood by the characters who are like me, and I am intrigued by the ones who think and respond so differently than I would. Their poor choices make me feel better about my own choices, and living vicariously through their triumphs spices up my life.

The danger zone is when I catch myself doing that with real people. I compare myself to someone else's Instagram feed, how much content they put out, how well they handle a situation, or how fast they rise to success. Then I feel second-rate. Before I learned to value my talents, when someone stepped into my scene with a stronger opinion or a louder voice, my initial instinct would be to defer to them. What I really wanted was to lead my own life with curiosity, openness, and quiet confidence.

Tension is part of any good story. Back when I was twenty, I thought twists and turns, a lack of answers, and uncertain plans meant I was failing in life. I couldn't have been more wrong: these twists and turns reveal who we are and what we're made of. Each one gives us an opportunity to learn, choose how we want to show up, and make sense of our goals, desires, and abilities. A good drama is more than its twists and turns. Our satisfaction comes from the protagonist's transformation—from naivety to maturity, from pride to humility, from hardness to compassion, from despair to redemption.

When I landed at that blank-slate place years ago, realizing I could live anywhere, go anywhere, and be anything, I stopped looking for answers for a while. My quest for a sense of significance retreated to the background. Somehow, I knew I couldn't do anything from my own emptiness. Feeling like God had brought me to this place, I let Him lead me to the next leg of my journey.

As in fictional stories, what moves our lives forward from scene to scene to the ultimate object of desire is either purposeful action or revelation. Sometimes "action" means taking any step from the situation we're in, even if we don't know the rest of the plan. We usually want the certainty of having the revelation first—that magical new piece of information that will unlock all the clarity we've been looking for. However, in taking a step, we get a different perspective, positioning us for the next scene in our story.

After that toxic friend and I moved out of our apartment, even though she was still in my life, being alone more and not working full-time gave me the stillness to simply be. The first step to finding my way was remembering who I was—and appreciating it.

Dare to Become Who Your Dream Needs You to Be

Imagine it's your funeral. The people you loved and impacted have gathered to tell the story of your life.

What kind of story do you want them to share?

What kind of inspiration have you been to the people in your life?

What accomplishments have impacted them?

Who have you become through the journey?

PART II

THE CALL

5

CHOOSE YOUR CHARACTER:
Remembering What Makes You *You*

*"The direction you are currently traveling—relationally,
financially, spiritually—will determine where you end up
in each of those respective arenas. This is true regardless of
your goals, your dreams, your wishes, or you wants. Your
current direction will determine your destination."*[8]

—Andy Stanley, pastor and author

I f you don't understand and accept who you are now,
comparison will steal the thrill of thriving in your story.
It looks at the movie trailer of someone else's life—all
the best parts—and compares it to the bloopers of your life.
Its reviews jab you where you're most vulnerable.
Why did that work for her and not me?
I should be farther in my career than I am.
I wish my life looked more like his.
You find yourself donning the mask of the person others
want you to be (or, at least, who you think they want you to
be). Doing the things that you think you should, you post

the best highlights and hide the ones that don't match your ideal. Betrayed, the real you feels lost and inadequate, and your voice is muffled.

How do you recognize the true you so you can play the lead role in your own story instead of the best friend?

Except for a couple weekly therapy sessions with my autistic client, which somehow made me feel alive again, I spent the next few months off work. With all that time to rest and reflect, I cracked open the window from what felt like an empty shell of a person, blinking against the light. Accepting the lie that I was insignificant and inconsequential had led me to become who others wanted me to be. It's no wonder it felt like there was little left of me.

So, who was I?

I remembered the scrapbook I had created of my Discipleship Training School experience the week after I came back. During our last week together, the students wrote encouraging messages in each other's notebooks. I had pasted each one in the back of my scrapbook. I hunted it down and read one after the other.

Each note displayed unique handwriting, reflecting the writer's personality. Tiny print with i's dotted with hearts. Flowing, neat cursive. Scrawling script. Slanted letters, sturdy letters, unkempt letters. Even the voice of each note brought countless memories of heart-to-heart conversations, tearful wrestling, and curious observations. The words of my bunkmate and newfound friend made me smile.

"Your mind really challenges me, and our *discussions* have been great. Thank you for your *genuineness* and *zeal* for our Father. I really see a *servant's heart* in you, and I admire that." —Julia

Of course, it was reassuring to remember what my closest friends saw in me. What about those with whom I hadn't connected as deeply? As I read note after note, themes began to stand out to me.

"The *servant heart* you so openly display really *helped* to encourage me to strive to be a servant. Thank you for the little words of *encouragement* you would drop my way. You always *seemed to know* just what I was needing to be lifted up." —Kelly

"I love the *gentle presence* you bring when you walk into a room. I love the way every once in a while, you totally *surprise* all of us by going totally *wild*!" —Tessa

"Thank you for our *talks* and your *honest, stable advice.* You are a young lady striving to be a *woman of God.* You *know what is important* and don't let other things cloud that. That is such an admirable trait." —Erica

Like water spilling through a dry and cracked riverbed, those words soaked life into my soul. Maybe I had connected more than I thought. Now I was curious. What had the leaders seen in me beyond all the times I slipped into introverted observation mode?

"I truly enjoyed your 'twisted' sense of *humor.*" —Brian

"You are such a great example of a *mature* young lady that is *secure in her identity* and understands who she is and where she comes from. Your *calm spirit* has been a blessing." —Udo & Ines

Tears burned my eyes. Had I really been all those things? I ached to be that girl again.

35

In a staff prayer time near the end of the program, while praying for and writing cards to the students, one word resonated for each student. The note in their card to me said, "We have seen your faithfulness." When I read over that two years later, a wave of grateful relief mingled with guilt and shame swept over me, and I sobbed. The girl who felt so invisible, like an outsider, had been seen. But the last thing I had been the past year was faithful.

Desperate to find that girl again, I revisited each description of me. Quiet. Calm-spirited. Steady. Open. Humourous. Sensitive to the Holy Spirit. Servant-hearted. Caring. Listener. Encourager. Example.

I wanted that to be me again—the best me, how God had made me. Daring to believe those things about myself again, I pulled each note out a second time and considered the words.

A quiet, gentle spirit—and that's a good thing. Yes, people might talk over me, overlook me, or underestimate me, but that's why it's such a gift to others. It's that nature that draws me into God's presence.

Steady and calm. This too helps me tune in to God's nudges. Even when I don't feel steady or calm on the inside, others still sense it when things get confusing or chaotic.

Open to new things God wants to show me. Though I feel resistant and frustrated in uncertainty, my openness invites new perspectives.

I have a quirky sense of humour. Even though I'm serious, I have a fun side. I like that about me, and others do too.

Through a swampy jungle of lies and self-doubt, these words helped me find my way back to who I was created to be.

Many of the attributes mentioned were qualities I had neglected or compromised—servant-heartedness, faithfulness, honesty, gentleness. Questioning whether my values were strong enough for me to get ahead in life, I veered from my connection to God. My servant-heartedness turned into people-pleasing. Assuming responsibility turned into codependency. My desire for goodness and fun turned into rebellion. When you compromise your true self and undermine your values, you lose trust in yourself. Without trust, deeper connections cannot grow, whether it's with others, God, or yourself.

GRIEVING A FRAGILE IDENTITY

When your sense of identity is attached to something fragile in life—a role, a job, your performance, what others say about you—it can make a crossroads feel extra daunting.

> When your sense of identity is attached to something fragile in life—a role, a job, your performance, what others say about you—it can make a crossroads feel extra daunting.

Sarah was a stay-at-home mom for years. Through all the challenges and fulfillment of raising her three daughters, she loved motherhood and saw it as her calling. Parenting became part of her identity, so the year her last daughter moved away for university, Sarah felt lost. She had done the best she could to prepare her daughters for adulthood, but she hadn't expected to feel so worried and empty when they left the nest. While her other friends were making travel and exploring career opportunities with their newfound freedom, she found herself going through the motions of deep cleaning her house and reading the stacks of books on her nightstand. Considering these were things she had always said she would do when the kids moved out, why did they feel so meaningless?

Dale was a high school science teacher for twenty-one years. It wasn't easy to keep students motivated and interested in his class, but he took it seriously. Over the years, however, shifting bureaucracy, budget cuts, and pressure to keep up with changes stirred up frequent heated conversations with his colleagues. The conflict took its toll on his mental health.

Taking a leave of absence helped for a while, but when he went back, panic attacks began. Finally, he resigned. Others called it early retirement, which didn't sit well with him. He had so much more to contribute, but who would want his ideas and expertise if they thought he was outdated and couldn't handle pressure?

If you've immersed yourself in one role for the last season, you need to grieve the end of one season to make space for another. The old role doesn't define you or your potential. A dimension of your complexity, it's part of your human-ness.

When pain, shame, and busyness overshadow us, it's hard to imagine life any other way. All we want to do is escape or numb it. Perhaps you wonder if you'll ever find the freedom to discover and express who you are, unaffected by what others think. As we mature, setbacks and losses in life can lead us to a crossroads of enlightenment. We realize the rationalizations and rhythms we relied on before are too constricting to serve us in our next season. Accepting how our experiences have shaped us, we invite a new chapter of becoming—ready or not.

Conflict and roadblocks still await us. The more confident we are in our capacity for growth, the more aware we are of our blind spots, and the more prepared we'll be to face resistance.

Dare to Remember What Makes You *You*

How do you recognize the best of who you are so you can appreciate your true self again? How well can you articulate who you are? Here are some tools that might help you.

- **Complete a personality questionnaire** such as Myers-Briggs, which is great for understanding how you think, make decisions, refuel, and interact with life, as well as how you relate to others.

- **Explore the Enneagram.** A tool for greater self-awareness and personal transformation, this personality typing doesn't put you in a box but instead helps you see how you view life. It reveals the primary desire and fear driving you and can steer you from the unhealthy to healthy parts of yourself.

- **Look back** on past report cards, reviews, testimonials, and journal entries for positive words others used to describe you.

- **Ask people you trust** (as well as those who don't know you well) to share a word or sentence to describe you. If the words they choose are attached to negative associations for you, separate them from that context and write down five aspects you appreciate about the quality.

6

COMBAT THE GREMLINS:
Recognizing Resistance
That Activates Courage

"Every creative person, and I think probably every other person, faces resistance when they are trying to create something good . . . The harder the resistance, the more important the task must be."

—Donald Miller, *A Million Miles in a Thousand Years*

You've had enough common sense and wisdom to get yourself this far in life. So, you wonder, why are you stuck now?

Why is it such a struggle to figure out this shift in your life, a shift that seems so much easier for everyone else?

Perfectionism and black-and-white thinking permeated my outlook well into my twenties. I had this expectation that everything should go smoothly in life. If something didn't, it must have been someone's fault, and it had to be fixed. If it was my fault, it meant there was something wrong with me.

Despite my compassionate and gentle nature, those high expectations meant I could be pretty judgmental towards others.

Writing became my playground for perfecting the world. Real people were messy, their issues too complicated for me to fix. The ones who seemed to have their life together weren't inviting me into their world, so I felt overlooked. In the scenes I wrote, characters invited me into their world and let me shape their unfortunate circumstances until things worked out.

I felt giddy when I daydreamed about these scenes. So, why didn't my precious scenes work well in the story that played through my imagination? Something was missing. I pored over books on writing fiction to find out why my books weren't as compelling as the published books on my shelf.

Huh, I thought as it started to make sense. *There's more to a page-turning book than relatable characters doing exciting things.*

GREMLINS AND VILLAINS

In the 1920s British air force pilots kept having inexplicable mishaps while they were in flight. Even after full ground inspections, while in the air their wings would tip the wrong way, mechanicals problems would surface, and even wires seemed to have been cut when nobody was looking. By World War II it was common for pilots to blame mischievous mythical creatures they called "gremlins" for the mysterious happenings.[9]

A fighter pilot named Roald Dahl had an unfortunate crash landing in a desert. He suffered a smashed skull and injured back, and it was months before anyone heard from him. After the war Dahl drew on this experience when he wrote his first of many novels for children. This book, *The Gremlins*, later became the movie that stirred up popularity about gremlins outside the air force world. Gremlins gradually entered our culture's vocabulary to allude to invisible things that cause trouble, bring inexplicable difficulties, and multiply like crazy.[10]

When it comes to conflict, we want something to blame. We need to wrap our mind around it and objectify it to defeat it.

I began to understand that conflict was necessary to create a compelling story, and without it I had nothing to propel my characters out of their comfort zones toward the climax.

Maybe I need a villain, I thought.

So, I added a creepy ex-con named Lane to my novel and gave him claim to treasure my protagonist, Diana, needed to save her family's farm. Discovering they had competition forced Diana and her best friend to do things they never would have thought to do otherwise. Putting these girls in a graveyard at night and making them break into Lane's home to search for clues made for fun scenes. But something still didn't jibe. I hadn't really intended to write a drama, nor a thriller. I hadn't even thought of my main characters as heroes. But adding a villain was the only way I could think of to add conflict to my young adult adventure story.

It wasn't until years of working through conflict and resistance in my own life that I realized a villain was only one form of conflict. Conflict shows up internally, not just externally. It bumps into our attitudes, upturns peaceful situations, and challenges our well-laid plans.

Before storytelling became a buzz word in marketing and personal growth arenas, I was using it to face fear and conflict at my crossroads.

Except I called it "adventure" and didn't realize it till years later.

Only working a couple hours a week and living in a temporary place with an unhealthy friendship, it felt like my life had come to a standstill at age twenty.

Usually passive, I knew my life needed a significant shift, and it wasn't going to happen on its own. Though I didn't know what career to pursue, what school to attend, or what direction to point my life, I did know it was time to get a different job. A friend told me she knew someone who found employment in a hotel in Banff, a tourist town nestled in the Rocky Mountains of Alberta.

"It's easy to get a job there," she said. "If you live in town, everything is within a fifteen-minute walk, so you don't even need wheels."

After months of riding my bike forty-five minutes to and from a two-hour shift (or depending on rides from my mom, who had to drive out of her way to drop me off), this appealed to me. I couldn't get the idea out of my head.

I told my mom, half expecting her to dismiss the idea so she could keep her eldest closer to home. People-pleasing had already become a gremlin in my life. Had she said it wasn't a good idea, I might not have gone. I didn't have much else going for me, so why trust my judgment now?

"Maybe you need a geographical change," she said. My mom's a wise woman. If she was willing to encourage her eldest to move away again, I figured there must be something to this idea.

I searched for job postings in Banff and found housekeeping positions galore. (A job where I didn't have to deal with people? I was *so* ready for that.) If I didn't have a direction for my life, I could at least gain some new experiences while I figured it out.

Within weeks my family drove across the province and through the magnificent Rocky Mountains to deliver me, my suitcase, and my two bins to my staff accommodations in Banff.

My thirteen months there were chock-full of new experiences. I dated a guy for the first time . . . and had my first breakup. While that conflict didn't feel great, it was nothing compared to living with a houseful of seven international strangers, negotiating for a time on one landline to fit conflicting time zones. (Cell phones weren't even a consideration then.) I chose to stand at a payphone for half an hour in -12°C (6°F) temperatures rather than face the glares of my housemates. Any kind of confrontation roused the taunts of the perfectionist gremlin:

> *You've been measured and rejected.*
> *You aren't worthy of being understood.*
> *You're too inadequate to hold your ground in a conversation.*

Since confrontation caused my whole body to shake and made me want to throw up, I avoided it at all costs.

The tension got so bad that I applied for a housekeeping job at another hotel. Within a month my kindhearted boss promoted me to supervisor—not because I was popular or exceptional at my work but because I was so slow and particular that no one wanted to work with me. Thankfully, I didn't find out the real reason until much later. The promotion was a much needed boost to my confidence.

The people I met at work intrigued me enough. I didn't care that they called me "Churchy" behind my back. Most of the young adults that streamed into Banff came to work, ski, and then party till they showed up hungover and miserable for work the next morning. Their lifestyle was unappealing enough to me that the people-pleasing gremlins didn't even try to talk me into fitting in with them. Instead, I was the oddball who went home after work to read books. Walking down unfamiliar streets below Cascade Mountain, content to absorb the majesty from below rather than on the ski slopes and hiking trails, was enough adventure for me.

Aside from colourful coworkers and roommate tension every few months when my rooming situation changed, the gremlins I faced were internal. Guilt and shame over regrets from the past haunted me. These gremlins thrive in secrecy and darkness, and I knew I wouldn't be able to see a new future until I exposed them to light. I summoned the courage to call and confess my ugly secrets to a close friend and my sisters. They tempered their reactions well and responded with compassion. Sharing with safe people made me feel stronger and shrunk the gremlins.

Facing the self-hatred gremlin was ten times worse. *You don't deserve a new dream*, it would tell me. *God gave you a heart and the opportunity to help people, and you screwed it up.* In my books you clean up your own mess, carry your own weight, and accept the consequences. Grace and forgiveness were words you talked about in church and at Bible studies. I had no idea what those words really meant until I needed them so desperately.

DEFEATED

Every day I cracked open my Bible to read a passage. I didn't do it with the same eagerness I had done for years before my season of disillusionment. Most days I felt numb and lost. But at one time I had felt close to God and considered Him my best friend, and I wanted to feel that again. I clung to the hope that reading the Bible would help.

The day I came to John 19, I almost skipped it. Already feeling despondent, it seemed like reading about Jesus being mocked and crucified wasn't going to be very inspiring.

But that day the passage came alive in slow motion.

Jesus's body convulsed under the whip laced with animal bone. Lash after lash, I cringed. Bright blood oozed from His wounds. Before He could gather himself, a soldier shoved thorns on His head.

"No!" I cried silently, tears streaming. I'd had enough. This was someone who knew everything I had done and not done and loved me anyway. I couldn't watch Him be tortured, even if it was only in my mind's eye.

Pilate came out and flaunted Jesus in front of the crowd. "I do not find him guilty of any crime," Pilate announced. But foreseeing a potential riot, Pilate pulled Him in for a private conversation. Jesus stood confident in who He was and in His mission, neither defending nor confronting. From my experience I knew how hard that is to do. My admiration for Him grew.

Watching the next scenes play out broke me. Rejection caused by fear. Pain. Humiliation. Torturous death.

My helplessness.

I finally awoke to the truth. All this time I'd been trying to earn my way back into God's presence, which goes against everything He's about. All my striving for goodness and measuring up had never been enough, but it took carrying a load too heavy, a mess too big to clean up on my own, to crumple in defeat.

My Australian roommate was due back any minute. What if she walked in on me crying? That awkward thought was enough for me to pull myself together. I headed outside into the rain, sagging under the weight of an invisible backpack filled with my gremlins and my mess. As I wandered the streets in the dark, cool raindrops washed away my warm tears. Half an hour later, wetter but calmer, I emerged from self-pity and hopelessness to a vision that felt real.

Jesus was walking beside me in the rain.

I didn't want to look at Him, but I couldn't help it. His eyes, compassionate and loving, captivated me.

He held out his hand, palm up. "You don't need that anymore."

The weight of my burden intensified. I drew back. "But this is mine. You shouldn't have to carry it for me. You've done so much. It's my responsibility, my burden to bear." My voice broke despite my resolve to keep my stand.

His voice was soft and so full of love it hurt. "I already paid your price. You don't need to carry it any longer. But it's your choice."

I hesitated. The offer was so tempting, but this was my responsibility. It wasn't fair to let someone else take it. Yet, here was someone who didn't want my friendship for what He could take from me. He understood me and was willing to sacrifice for me—He already had. Isn't that what I had longed for? I imagined slipping the backpack off my shoulders, lurching as its weight dropped. I offered it to Him, and sadness deepened in His eyes as He accepted it. He slung it over His shoulders, and now His shoulders slumped under the weight. Tears from both our faces mingled with the rain. He wrapped His arm around me, and we walked.

It's not the imagery you usually hear about in church. I've encountered numerous sermons about grace where the pastor will have a cross at the front of the stage. Everyone would be invited to write the names of their mistakes and wounds on pieces of paper and come up to nail them to a cross. It's powerful and lifechanging for many people.

That day, God gave me the imagery I needed not only to acknowledge my helplessness but to accept His invitation to surrender. Without gremlins clamoring about and regret weighing me down like rocks, I felt incredibly light and peaceful as I walked back to my dorm. I still didn't know what paths lay ahead for me, and that was okay. Hope told me I would embark on new adventures soon enough.

Finding ourselves stalled out at a crossroads is the perfect time to name the gremlins in our lives.

For me, they were Perfectionism, Need for Acceptance and Approval, Shame, and Fear. I used tactics like Blame, Avoidance, and Try Harder to fight them off. Your gremlins and tactics might differ. They might wear you down, but your resilience will strengthen. As we'll see in the next chapter, fresh approaches to facing this resistance can bring anything from healing to collaboration to new dreams.

Dare to Face Your Villains and Gremlins

Below are common external sources of conflict you might find in novels or movies. Call these villains if you need to. Which kind are you up against?

Self vs self	Self vs someone else
Self vs nature / environment	Self vs technology / machines
Self vs society / systems	Self vs health / disease
Self vs the unknown	Self vs supernatural

Most of our villains in life are internal, not external. They might be interfering, sabotaging, distracting, or undermining you. Which ones have been holding you back?

Addiction	Lack
Apathy	Lies you believe
Beliefs	Low confidence
Character flaw	Naivety
Comfort	Need
Confusion	Obligation
Deflecting ownership	Passive Faith
Denial	Passivity
Expectations	People-pleasing
Fear	Perfectionism
Guilt	Regret
Hunger for acceptance	Scarcity mindset
Idealism	Self-doubt

Impostor syndrome   Self-sabotage
Impulsively   Shame
Insecurity

7

DREAM NEW DESTINATIONS:
Accepting the Gifts of
an Emerging Path

"If destiny didn't want me to be a writer
it shouldn't have made me one."

—Elizabeth Gilbert, author of *Eat, Pray, Love* and *Big Magic*

Where do you want to end up?

My adulthood has been salted with quotes like "Begin with the end in mind"[11] from Stephen Covey, known for his book *The 7 Habits of Highly Effective People.*

Whether you're tackling a big or small project, whether you're starting your day or a journey, this advice prompts us to visualize the outcome we want and work backward. When I knew the outcome and the steps to get there, I was effective and efficient.

But what about when I *didn't* know the outcome I wanted?

I felt the pressure to choose the right goal, or my entire life would be screwed up. I didn't want to pick just any path. I wanted a purpose, something meaningful to be a part of.

When we're stuck at a crossroads, our frustration rarely is about the intersection itself. It's about where we want to end up—or don't want to end up—and how we feel when life doesn't turn out the way we expect. For overthinkers it's not even about where you are now but the what-if as you consider what you might miss out on by choosing one path over the other.

Fear, over-analysis, and uncertainty made decision-making complicated. I wondered, had I felt more certain about my calling, would I have been more decisive in exploring my dreams? And on the other hand, was it okay if I enjoyed what I was doing behind the scenes? Or was I selling myself short in some way?

Maybe you're struggling with similar confusing questions:

Am I allowed to have this dream?
Is this God's will? How do I know?
Where can I contribute what I have to offer?
What if I choose the wrong path?
Did I hear God or choose right in the first place?
What if I don't want this dream anymore?

Often, we're too close to our own story to consider a different perspective. It's in others' stories that we recognize what we want or realize we're not the only ones grappling with this.

I felt this way a few years ago when I first discovered an online Christian yoga instructor named Caroline Williams. Through her yoga videos on YouTube, she invited my heart, soul, and body into God's presence, breaking through a season of spiritual numbness. When I discovered she had transitioned from politics to Christian yoga, it caught my attention.

What in the world would inspire a political go-getter to become a Christian yoga instructor?

I followed my curiosity and scoured Google and her social media history. Then, I asked her if I could interview her. To my delight, she agreed. When we chatted over a video call, she was warm and authentic, her smile welcoming, her simple New York apartment serving as the backdrop. Her story reminded me of a truth that had been dawning in my heart: having a dream, a clear path towards it, and the drive to make it happen might not mean as much as I thought it did.

WHAT IF I HAVE THE WRONG DREAM?

Caroline Williams graduated from high school knowing exactly what she wanted to do with her life. Her dream was to walk the halls of Congress. If you had told her that one day, yes, she would walk those halls, but she'd be wishing she were anywhere else, she wouldn't have believed you. If you then had told her she would one day be a Christian yoga teacher with over twenty-six thousand YouTube subscribers[12], she would have laughed at you.

Caroline was on a mission to change the world on a grand scale. Obviously, she assumed, working in government would allow her to have that kind of influence and authority. So confident was she in her mission, she had her career all planned out. Right after college, out of a long line of people vying to work with a certain congressman, she landed the job. Six months into working with the district office, through a crazy set of circumstances, the DC office offered her a position. She and her husband of six months packed up and moved to Washington DC.

This was the dream.

Until a month later when the unhappiness crept in.

Phone calls would come into her office. "If you don't renew my benefits, I can't pay for my groceries tomorrow," one lady told her in desperation. On the other end of the phone, Caroline felt helpless and frustrated, thinking, *I literally can do nothing for you here. I know it seems like I have the power to do something, but I really don't.*

This life seemed far from what had ignited her passion for politics.

"What I learned probably doesn't surprise you," she said, chuckling on our video call. "You really don't have that kind of influence on a big scale. It's quite frustrating and demoralizing, realizing what a big bureaucracy it is, and you quickly realize you're just one cog in the machine. It wasn't what I thought it was going to be. It felt so frustrating being that far removed from helping people on an individual level, which is where change starts."[13]

Caroline spent three years in Washington, DC living her dream in misery, wrestling with God.

God, I was so sure you had called me to this, she would pray over and over. *Have I missed something? Have I failed myself? Have I failed You?*

To further her frustration, God didn't seem keen on answering. All she wanted was clear direction. She wanted God to tell her something like, "Go to law school, then apply for a job at this place."

During that time she was doing all the things she thought a good Christian does. She read her Bible and prayed. She went to church and served there. Yet, she felt she wasn't getting anywhere with God. All the distractions of her ambitious mind and busy schedule didn't inspire much inner peace either.

Yoga classes unexpectedly offered solace. She felt a little wary at first, knowing yoga is controversial in Christian circles.[14] But the movement quieted her mind and made her feel grounded and healthy, so she trusted Jesus would meet her there.

One day, lined up with sweaty yogis crammed in the room around her, she stretched and flowed through positions to soothing music and the calm voice of the instructor. An hour later she lay on her mat in bliss. As stillness settled into breathing, she sensed a crescendo of God's presence.[15]

Do you have any idea how much I love you? Do you know how proud I am of you? she sensed Him say. Tears slipped down her cheeks into her ears. Snot pooled above her lip. In the drought of a heart thirsty to connect with and receive direction from God, the voice flooded the cracked soil of her soul. Her "body shook with the silent sobs of surrender."[16]

As the yoga teacher talked gently about being kinder to themselves, Caroline felt the studio thick with God's presence—deeper than she'd ever felt before except for a few church services.

She began meeting God on her yoga mat regularly. Somehow, showing up every week to a jam-packed studio created space for the Holy Spirit to overwhelm her with His presence. She could be present, move, and breathe. His gentle voice cut through the noise of her confusion and busy life. He connected with her heart.

"I remember thinking it would be so awesome to just do this with worship music and prayer," she told me as she reflected on that tumultuous yet profound season.[17]

The clues of a calling from God are often subtle. Like foreshadowing in an unfolding story, they are mysterious. We rarely see their significance until later.

Caroline kept waiting for her divine direction to map her way to a better job. But God seemed to be more interested in her healing and freedom than helping her navigate a tidy, quick path to a new, successful career. As she wrestled through a couple more years in politics, she kept meeting God on her mat. She began to realize how much her identity was wrapped in her idea of success and career.

Her misery begged to be acknowledged, but admitting she was unhappy would feel as if she had failed God and herself.

Finally facing that she was genuinely unhappy, Caroline conceded that she didn't want to climb the success ladder anymore. But what else could she do? She had no idea. All she could do was trust that this was the path she was on and that God had something more for her.

One day she stumbled onto an organization that offered Christian yoga teacher training.

Something inside her lit up.

She'd had no desire to be a yoga instructor. Such a dream had never once factored into her ideas of success. "I have no idea where this is going, but I just feel like this is something I have to do," she told her husband, who encouraged her to go for it.

Making that choice was her first step in understanding that God doesn't always speak to us through writing in the sky. We want the roadmap, the five-year plan, and absolute clarity to know our next step and when to take it. As we spoke, Caroline reflected. "You just have to trust that thing that lights you up and be willing to take a step in the dark. It's okay to be like, *I have no idea where this is going, but for some reason this excites me, and I have to say yes to it.*"[18]

WHEN DREAMS EMERGE

Some dreams grow with us as if they are part of our identity. We hardly know life without them. And the moment we're old enough, the moment we scrape together enough money or dare to believe in ourselves enough, we make them happen. Hunger for adventure drives us. Grit and passion propel us through obstacles.

For these dreams it's not a question of choosing a path. The dream just is. It's there, and we do it.

Other dreams come as a thousand-piece puzzle dumped out on a board, asking for assembly. We pick out pieces of the puzzle and fit patches together, starting with the edges. It's easier to know the boundaries of our dream—what framework of expectations, rules, and colours we have to work with. As we put patches of the puzzle together, a sinking feeling washes over us as we realize the puzzle doesn't match the picture we were given. We have no idea what the big picture is. Only by fitting the pieces together—standing back every so often to take it all in—will we catch glimpses of the vision.

Caroline finished her yoga instructor training, but she still was trying to figure out her career path. She would apply for jobs, but after five or six rounds of interviews, she never got an offer. She was banging on all these doors, and not one was opening. Her frustration with God mounted. He still wasn't being clear about where she was supposed to go.

One day her friend said, "Caroline, why don't you just quit your job?"

That was the lightbulb moment she needed. Of course, it had always been an option, but it never even crossed her mind to leave without having the next plan. Though she and her husband needed her income, she handed in her two weeks' notice.

Somehow, she knew she had to step out in faith.

Within days a colleague reached out to her. "Hey, I have a job for you here in Atlanta. Do you want to come?"

As Caroline related the story to me, she shook her head with a smile. "God knows. You take a step, and He's already there. He's already lined something up for you."[19]

IS IT A DREAM AWAY FROM OR TOWARDS SOMETHING?

We think the fruition of a big dream is what we're aiming for, that our peak of success is the climax of the story. Since it is desire that fuels our steps forward and pushes past barriers, there is merit to that.

But sometimes a dream is more about the urge to get away from something—a job, a relationship situation, a circumstance—than a vision we're running towards. It becomes a series of blind steps, an assembly of mini dreams weaving one into the other as we navigate the frustrations of the present. Discovering what you don't love anymore and who you don't want to be anymore is equally important as having something to chase after.

Having a big, new dream propels us toward a future filled with adventure and fulfillment. But what if the new path doesn't reveal itself because we're not ready for it?

We overlook the significance of how we bring ourselves into the dream journey.

Of course, we're in our own journey. But think about the significance of that. We bring along the way we see ourselves. What we believe about ourselves. The shame, the pain, the expectations we carry inside. We carry with us unexamined priorities. Chances are that many of these will fall short of what it takes to enter a new reality.

These things don't change on their own.

New phases of our calling require new versions of us. If someone were to wave a fairy godmother wand and plunk us into a dazzling new dream, I wonder if it would be setting us up for failure. Would it shock our system so much that we would become a danger to the sacred assignment? We would have a new environment, new responsibilities, and fresh opportunities. But how much would our old lenses and habits summon cycles of old realities? How much would the same approaches to our problems bring us the same results?

The dream beyond our crossroads, if it's alluring enough, makes the journey of transforming worth the pain and discomfort. Even an interim goal such as decluttering your home, signing up for a marathon, or taking on an exciting yet scary project invites you to begin the process of becoming who you would like to be on the other side of your crossroads.

I saw this threaded through Caroline's Instagram feed when she first started her yoga instructor training.

WELCOMING A DREAM THROUGH PRACTICE

Caroline and her husband eventually took stock of their unrealized dreams and moved to New York City. While she didn't have a new career mapped out, and only her husband had a job, they were ready for this new adventure. After months of deliberation, Caroline launched her Instagram feed, inviting others to her yoga journey. Her frustration with her career in politics fell to the background—at least to anyone looking in from the outside.

As God prepares to release us into a new adventure in His story, either before or while He's giving us a new assignment, He addresses our identity or our wholeness. Not so we're qualified for our dream or task. One only needs to look at the Bible to realize a calling isn't about qualifications. Its pages are peppered with imperfect, unqualified people who were invited into a role in God's mission. But God creatively uses our suffering, inadequacies, and brokenness to show us where our identity lies and what we look to for completeness.

> God creatively uses our suffering, inadequacies and brokenness to show us where our identity lies and what we look to for completeness.

For Caroline, the discipline of daily yoga practice increased her awareness that this journey wasn't about perfecting but rather about becoming. Training her body to twist, balance and stretch in new ways brought her face to face with her fears.

Soon she got brave and offered yoga classes, but no one showed up. It wasn't a surprise since she was still new and unknown in New York.

She regrouped, unable to deny that for some reason God wanted her to use yoga to lead people into His presence. She pushed her furniture to the walls in her tiny New York apartment, set up a camera in her closet, and recorded a yoga session. When she posted it on YouTube, she didn't know anything about sound mixing, lighting, or anything techy. This made her surrender every remaining fragment of her perfectionism. It was more of a step of obedience and a compelling in her heart than a dream yet.

She didn't even understand what it had to do with her purpose.

WHEN DREAMS ARE DAMPENED BY DISAPPOINTMENT

I love a beautifully wrapped gift. The shimmery, wrinkle-free paper. A tightly bound, evenly tied satin ribbon topped with a matching cascading bow. I'm as captivated by a beautiful present as my toddler was with the colourful box that held a new toy.

Every Christmas my relatives demonstrate how tantalizing giftwrapping can be. Each aunt, uncle, and cousin brings a wrapped gift and puts it in the centre of a large circle of chairs. One by one we choose a present either from the middle or by swiping it from someone's lap. The criteria behind the choice ranges from "prettiest parcel" to "noisiest rattle" to "someone else wants it." Rarely does the item inside reflect the nature of the gift once unwrapped.

Dreams are the pretty packaging that present your purpose.

You were lovingly designed for a purpose. Your Creator thoughtfully crafted together your personality, your passions and strengths. He placed you lovingly in your story and set your purpose in motion.

Some people's dreams reveal their purpose clearly, like a gift basket of wine and cheese wrapped in clear cellophane. Ever since they were young, their gifts and passions have been obvious, and they know exactly how they're going to use them to make the world a better place.

Other people uncover their purpose the way my sisters and I found a Christmas present too big to fit under the tree the year I was nine. We opened a simple present under the tree, which told us to find another wrapped clue. Hunting down that clue, then another, we finally ended up in my parents' closet squealing over a white doll crib my dad had made. Like this scavenger hunt, some people don't recognize their purpose until after they sift through the clues in their dreams, passions, and experiences.

We're multisensory beings, so the best dreams engage our emotions and paint a compelling picture. They give us a taste of what we might see, feel, or smell when the dream becomes reality. Unfortunately, even with planning and persistence some dreams don't turn out the way we imagined. With that reality comes disappointment—and hesitation to dream again. When all we see is negative, it's hard to spot hope, purpose, or character growth. Without hunger or passion to wake us up, we hit snooze and roll back over. Drudging through our daily tasks, we busy ourselves with the mundane, hoping clarity will present itself.

Even though Caroline connected with an increasing number of people through her YouTube channel and her New York classes gained momentum, she felt frustrated with the dream that was starting to unfold. Usually driven, she felt like a failure because of her uncertainty in how to move forward.

Finally, she brought all her messy feelings into the light. She opened her Bible and found herself reading Proverbs 16:26 (MSG): "Appetite is an incentive to work; hunger makes you work all the harder."

Sensing this was the truth she needed, she opened her journal to a fresh page and wrote, *God, give me your appetite for this dream. I don't want to work harder out of guilt or performance but only in response to love and the appetite you stir in me.*[20]

That weekend, ideas and enthusiasm overflowed for her yoga influence and the higher calling in her life.

Over the next years she settled into a yoga studio space, offered yoga retreats around the world, launched a successful Kickstarter campaign to fund a filming project, and started The Abbey, an online community of people who use yoga to connect to the loving heart of God.[21]

Oh, and somewhere in there she finally left her political career to live her new dream full-time.

What if you've stalled at your crossroads because you've withheld permission from yourself to invest in your dream?

What if you're scared that you'll choose the wrong path? What if you don't have clarity or hunger for your dream anymore?

Caroline summed this up beautifully towards the end of our video chat.

"How are you different now than when you were twenty, having been through this journey?" I asked.

"I think I am a lot less panicked than I was about purpose, identity, and path," she told me with a peaceful smile. "That felt like everything to me in my twenties. What I did for work was so core to who I was. That felt huge, and I've honestly let that go. What I'm doing now, I really love it. I feel fulfilled.

It feels like an act of obedience. But in five years I may be doing something totally different. And that's okay, too. I think I grew up with the understanding that God's written out the story of your life . . . He guides every one of your steps, and while that's true, it registered in my brain as, 'Stay on the one path. Do not mess up. Do not make the wrong decision about which way to go.' I've learned, at least in the way God has developed a relationship with me, that He trusts me with a lot of those decisions. And I think I'm ready to trust myself with them and trust that if I'm going down the wrong road, He'll make it known."[22]

Dare to Awaken Your Dream

Journal what you sense is your emerging path. Write as if no one will read it. Give yourself permission to be curious about the possibilities. What dream or ideas have been calling to you? What could it look like if they became reality? What would feel energizing? How would it sound? Feel? Look? Who would benefit, and how?

8

DESIRE THAT DRIVES YOU:
Uncovering the Force That Nudges You Forward

"Authenticity is a collection of choices that we have to make every day. It's about the choice to show up and be real. The choice to be honest. The choice to let our true selves be seen."

—Brené Brown, *The Gifts of Imperfection*

"Aghhh," I growled at my computer screen.

Stuck again. I was working on the novel that had been living in my imagination for years. After the writers in my critique group informed me that my protagonist was flat and unrealistic, I spent the week trying to figure out what to do about it. I wanted to create the connection that thrilled me when I read a well-crafted novel. I wanted characters that came alive.

I knew my character inside and out. Diana was a spunky, say-it-like-it-is young adult who wanted freedom to live life on her terms without the instability of people's plans changing. But when my critique group read through it, they ripped apart my character and writing with as much straight-shooting spunk as Diana. She came across immature and naive when I meant to portray zest with attitude. With a sigh I turned off my computer and prepared to attend a monthly workshop for writers.

That night at our local library, the presenter talked about the difference between *directional desire* and the *deeper desire* that propels a character.

"In every story the main character needs to want something," she told us. "Maybe she wants to plan the perfect wedding. Maybe he wants to save his kidnapped daughter. The more specific the desire, the easier it will maintain the focus of the character through the story. A vague desire will snuff out the story."

No wonder I'm stuck, I thought. *Diana's desire isn't clear enough to keep my story moving.*

"But you need more than that," the instructor went on. "With only this directional desire, it will seem like a mechanism to manipulate the character through a predictable series of scenes. The deeper desire—this inner motivation, the complex need in us—demands to be satisfied. It's *why* the directional desire matters so much, yet it's usually the need that gets in the way of what she wants. A protagonist might want to plan the most beautiful wedding ever because she longs to feel like a cherished princess, and this might be the closest she ever gets. In her hunger for affirmation, she accommodates every family member's preference for the wedding. When family members start yelling at each other and turning on her, she somehow must find different ways to fill her need for acceptance before she can have the confidence to pull together the wedding she actually wants. The deeper desire both complicates and drives her through the plot."

The two tiers of desire made sense to me, both for my story and for real life.

We are complicated humans with paradoxical desires that both undermine and drive the things we need and want. I made the mistake of using my novel as a chance to clean up life and polish the perfection I had been striving for. In the process I stole the very thing that humanized Diana and would have drawn readers to connect with her.

DESIRE: WHAT DO YOU REALLY WANT, AND WHY?

Which desires do you find easier to identify? Is it easy to choose directional desire, which determines what you want to be when you grow up or what project you'll immerse yourself into next? Or do you know the deeper desire you want to fulfill, yet the best tangible goal eludes you?

I think back to my twenty-year-old self and my twenty-six-year-old self before my life collapsed into burnout. My confidence peaked when I had a concrete mission, whether it was the course I was saving up for or the work project I had to tackle. But when I didn't know to process my *deeper desires*—my need to be known and seen for me, not what I could do for others—and integrate them with a tangible path, I would inevitably collapse into disillusionment. Had someone regularly sat down with me, provided a safe space for me to babble, and then gently spoken what I needed to hear—oh, the peace and clarity I might have felt!

My younger self was aching to hear someone with compassion and understanding say something like this:

I see you.

I see your quiet reserve, your dedication to doing your best. I see your eagerness to serve others so they're free to do what's important to them. When it comes to the moments that matter, you have the resolve of an oak tree. Though storms rage around you, you can stand firm and offer a shelter of hope.

You think you are reserved, but I see your calm quiet as a beacon of assurance. Your quiet confidence brings peace and inspiration to others' inner storms.

But things are choking out that beautiful identity. You're a sponge for the approval of others. You've banished yourself to the sidelines and shrunk into invisibility because you believe someone else can do it better than you. You're entrapped by excuses.

You wish someone would tell you what to want and what to dream. But you were created with dreams already inside you.

You are a masterpiece that will inspire other beautiful masterpieces. You're looking for approval? You have mine. Go for it. You're aching to be good enough, but if you dwell on it, that ache will never go away.

Just go for it.

How would your heart respond if someone sincerely looked you in the eyes and spoke those words to you?

The thing is, along the way certain people did say pieces of that to me. Some of those words I clung to. Others bounced off me because I couldn't see it. What was that about? What could have steered me out of that mess?

What would propel *you* out of doubt and insecurity?

Maybe it would help to have a better understanding of the kinds of desires that emerge in life.

DIRECTIONAL DESIRES

In the simplest form, a directional desire could be a goal, a way to fill your time, or a means to make money. It refers to the pull towards a tangible object, accomplishment, or role you want.

When you're feeling stuck in figuring out a directional desire, often the oversimplified solution offered is to "find your passion." Of course, if you know the one thing you were passionate about above everything else, it's probably already pulling you in that direction. Or maybe you have so many thrilling ideas that you're not sure where to focus.

What if you're like many people I've met who are frustrated that there's not one thing compelling them over another? *Passion* seems like too strong a word to reflect the levels of desire they have, so they have no idea how to choose one direction over another. That's when it's worth considering the following levels of intensity of what delights or disturbs you.

- **Interest** is the birthplace for desire; it is what awakens your attention enough to learn more about something.

- **Curiosity** is a desire to pursue an understanding not yet satisfied. It motivates you to dispel uncertainties, grow knowledge, and mature your perspective. Curiosity listens and uncovers doors to potential passion.

- **Passion** is ongoing enthusiasm for something or someone. It fuels your energy. It means caring about an issue so much that you keep pressing through misunderstandings and obstacles. It spurs you out of your comfort zone and onto your journey, catching the attention of people around you.

- **Hunger** is a full-throttle drive that throws you into something wholeheartedly. It immerses you into learning everything you can. It turbocharges you forward. It plows through obstacles. It catapults you past your fears, cuts through excuses, and creates new rules for living. It helps you bounce back after failure if you don't let disappointment keep you down.

We'll explore how the things that delight or disturb you can help you figure out your directional desire in chapter thirteen. For now, let's look at deeper desires.

Deeper Desires

These internal desires—we'll call them "core needs"—influence how you see and respond to the paths at your crossroads. These are underlying yearnings and needs that must be met for you to thrive as a creative, vibrant, healthy person. They make you human. Left unfulfilled or temporarily satisfied with false promises, you feel displaced or broken. Fulfilled, you feel whole and generous.

CORE NEEDS: WHY DO YOU WANT IT?

Discovering the essence of your "why" heightens your awareness to see with a new perspective not only your desires but also your detours and obstacles.

Plenty of psychologists have developed theories over the years about what inner needs need to be met for us to meet our full potential. Many people can explain those theories better than I. Leadership coach Tony Stoltzfus[23] explains this in a way that revolutionized my awareness of these desires in my own life. With over three thousand hours invested in coaching leaders towards finding purpose in their pain and maximizing their impact and growth during difficult seasons, his research identifies sixteen foundational yearnings we all have:[24]

Achievement Desires: justice, challenge, significance, freedom
Connection Desires: worth, distinction, joy, love
Stability Desires: belonging, comfort, security, peace
Competence Desires: come through, goodness, recognition, approval[25]

Remember earlier when I wrote what I would have said to my twenty-year-old self? Over the years people did say bits and pieces of that. I clung to those words of encouragement, and they boosted my spirits for a time. But there were times when only the One who created me could still my storm inside and speak gentle words of authority. He nourished me with His goodness and approval. Anything else was counterfeit—empty calories that left me craving more.

When I felt invisible, aching to be seen and heard, it felt exhausting and frustrating. It felt like fighting for a place in the conversation around a dinner table of peers. But I slowly discovered that when I went to Jesus first with my hunger, I could show up in the same dinner conversation with the gentle confidence I wanted to present. Often, my desire for purity and goodness was mistaken for perfectionism and legalism. I gradually matured as I experienced grace in different areas of my life. Whenever I went to God in prayer or in my journal and let Him affirm my desire for goodness, I could receive correction more easily.

It feels vulnerable to acknowledge your deepest desires when you've guarded them so fiercely. It's humbling to realize when you can't fill those needs on your own. But when you truly uncover your core desires and acknowledge what can fulfill them—and what cannot—the weight you've been carrying diminishes. As your expectations shift, you release your grip on what you thought would make all the difference, and the adventure begins.

I'm not sure what your view of God is or what your experience with Him has been, but I hope you're open to a new adventure. Some people approach God like He's a takeout drive-thru or a taskmaster who only cares about what we do. When we realize God created us to desire and that those desires were meant to be filled within relationship with God, everything changes.

It did for me.

READY FOR A NEW ADVENTURE

When my employment contract was up in Banff, I knew it was time to move on.

Thirteen months prior I had arrived a shell of the girl I once knew, doubting my judgment and consumed by shame. Now, I felt restored by God's immense love and grace. The majestic mountains became a symbol of God's presence, which strengthened me. Conversations with coworkers opened my perspective on other worldviews. These conversations solidified what I valued—my faith, solitude, meaningful dialogue, sobriety, and work ethic. They also reaffirmed what I had no interest in—loud parties, self-deception, and coming across as an unapproachable religious good girl.

One by one as work contracts finished, our team of housekeepers was replaced by other thrill-seeking skiers and snowboarders. With his usual friends gone, one coworker started hanging out with me a little more. We had been oil and water before. He was the favourite, the life of the party with the kind of humour that forced you to take yourself less seriously. I was the austere, "churchy" supervisor who didn't let the housekeepers get away with mediocre work. Restless after hours of reading alone, I would drop by his staff accommodations, sending him and his roommate scrambling to hide things they didn't want the "good girl" to know about. When boredom prompted me to hang out with them in the hotel hallways, I could tell they didn't know what to do with me.

As we walked to and from work and dragged out our tasks during the slow season, he gradually allowed me past his funny façade. More than once he admitted that watching me hold fast to my values and considering my questions had challenged him to evaluate his own beliefs and goals.

His contract ended two months before mine. As we hugged goodbye before he boarded the bus, I noticed how choked up he was. The bus drove off, leaving me feeling both empty and hopeful. Empty because I wasn't sure if I was losing a friend and because a season was ending. Hopeful because somehow, by being my awkward self, unmoving yet compassionate, I had helped someone find hope and meaning for their life. That meant the world to me. I hadn't done it alone. I did it by first finding my acceptance, courage, and security in God. It felt like redemption.

I was ready for my next adventure, and I still had to decide where I would move. But with this new approach to life, my trust in Him would deepen with each stretching experience. When life yet again didn't turn out the way I wanted, I would still be able to salvage hope. Amid the uncertainty of what was next, I could find peace.

Dare to Uncover Your Deeper Desire/Core Need

Think back to a decision you had to make. What was the directional desire—the accomplishment you were aiming for? What was your deeper desire—the core need?

Now, think about one of the directional desires you're currently contemplating. What's the deeper desire—the core need—behind why you're considering that direction?

PART III

THE COMPASS

9

SET YOUR COMPASS

When we're not sure what our dream destination look is, a GPS approach hurts us more than it helps us. We get caught up in whether we're on the right path, rather than finding the adventure from where we are.

—Emily Grabatin

I was nine when my dad showed me how to use a compass. He knew a thing or two about compasses. As a forester he would often be dropped off on the side of a mountain by helicopter, or he might drive along logging roads that weren't on any maps. So, when my Pioneer Club friends had to work on our orienteering badges, my dad showed us a few tips. He explained that the earth has a magnetic field, and it has a north pole and a south pole like both ends of a magnet, which can either click together or repel one another. That wasn't very interesting . . . until we saw how the magnetic needle would stay in one spot no matter which way we rotated the compass. No matter where we were or how many of the trees around us looked the same, we could figure out where north was. And if we had a map and a few instructions, knowing where north was could help us figure out where we needed to go. Now it was time to try it out. Forget crossroads—he sent us on a scavenger hunt in the woods, and the only way we would find our prizes was to use the compass to follow his directions.

After years of using maps and never needing a compass, I used a GPS for the first time. It felt like cheating, listening to a voice tell me exact directions instead of stopping at the side of the road to consult a map. If I wanted to choose an alternate route ahead of time, it was helpful to know which way would be faster or have better gas mileage. The only trouble, the GPS wasn't very flexible on the go. If I had to take a detour or missed a turn, it kept directing me in circles, trying to get me back onto the exact route it had mapped out for me. Still, now that I'm used to it, I rarely leave home without it.

Often, we expect a GPS-led life. We want to know our exact destination and the exact steps it takes to get there. And that sure is helpful when you know where you're going and how the GPS settings work. It also helps when the coordinates are actually in the GPS's programming so you don't end up in a rural dead end. But when the path doesn't turn out the way we expect, we have a hard time knowing how much to trust the directions or how to adapt. When we're not sure what our destination is, a GPS approach hurts us more than it helps us. We get caught up in whether we're on the right path rather than finding the adventure right where we are.

At a Dare to Decide crossroads, you'll benefit more from the inner compass approach.

Having a Divine-inspired purpose narrows your focus in a particular direction. An openness to adventure strengthens your resolve and adaptability. An adventure mindset grows the confidence you'll blossom through your experiences. Core values guide how you'll go about the journey. Priorities and principles offer discernment for managing what's most important along the way. In the coming chapters we'll explore these in more depth.

When my dad held a magnet near his compass, the needle yanked toward the magnet regardless of where north was. Imagine being in the middle of an adventure with a skewed sense of direction. Who knows where you would end up?

When you realize you're not where you thought you were, you feel disoriented, stressed, and out of control. Your mind either freezes or spins. Conflicted, you may feel torn between competing priorities. You're drained from a schedule crammed with obligations, but you have no idea what you've accomplished. And regret over things you've done in the past unsettles you.

How can you figure out what's most important to you amid magnetic pulls of expectations, obligations, and busyness? Let's discern your inner compass, starting by demagnetizing any myths you believe about your purpose.

Dare to Set Your Inner Compass

Can you remember a time when you were more focused on the steps to get somewhere than enjoying the adventure of it? How did this help you? What did you miss out on because of having a GPS approach?

10

MYTHS OF PURPOSE:
Lies That Hold You Back

*"Sometimes . . . our most powerful learning happens
not so much in the moment we find the answer, but in
the moment we're willing to pursue the questions."*

—Erwin McManus

At a crossroads, an underlying enigma arises. For some, not knowing which career is the "right" one induces tearful panic. Others feel frozen with the fear that they've messed up God's will for their life. It's an existential question that pops up in churches, counselling clinics, blogs, and research studies. It haunted me in my twenties.

The question sounds different depending on the circumstance.

Will I ever feel alive and fulfilled in life? Sylvia wondered. As a dreamer with ambitious goals, she worked hard to see her dreams come true. When she crashed from discouragement and a health crisis, she wasn't sure what to hope for anymore.

What's my contribution in life now that I'm retired? Dan asked as the novelty of sleeping in and being home all day wore off. After decades of feeling fulfilled and validated by his role as a teacher, retirement wasn't all it was cracked up to be. He found himself bored or busy with nothing to show for it.

Crystal had built a successful business. Things were rolling smoothly, and the money was coming in. With the freedom she now had to step away and travel or simply enjoy life, an unsettling emptiness crept into the quiet moments. She found herself asking, *Why am I here on earth? Why do I exist?*

How do I find my passion? Allison journaled, trying to relieve the stress after getting her student loan bill. It was hard enough choosing her major in college. After hundreds of hours in school, thirty-grand in debt, and minimum-wage job offers, she now realized this wasn't the fulfilling life she had prepared for.

Is there more to life than this? Tracy wondered while she changed her one-year-old's diaper and cleaned up spilled cereal as her three-year-old threw a tantrum. As much as she loved her kids, she felt ashamed to admit she didn't enjoy being a mom. She felt tired all the time. Getting out of the house was such a hassle, so she didn't go anywhere. She felt isolated and depressed and then felt guilty for feeling that way.

What was the point of that hell I went through? Jack had spent the last ten years in survival mode. He felt wrung out after a nasty custody battle and the shrinking world of his life as a single dad. After a heart-wrenching year of watching his mom fight cancer, the funeral was behind him, and now life was settling into a more predictable rhythm. But that one question kept badgering him.

Maybe one of these questions is the core of your crossroads conundrum. Perhaps you thought you only needed to choose between a couple of paths when all the while your heart has been asking a much bigger question:

What's my purpose in life?

Viktor Frankl obsessed about this concept when he ended up in a Nazi concentration camp. His thesis manuscript was confiscated soon after he was imprisoned. He was devastated to lose his work but found opportunities to observe and help people find meaning, even in the most gruesome circumstances.[26]

Once, he encountered a man contemplating a way to escape his torment. Frankl told him, "If you commit suicide, you'll rob yourself of an amazing opportunity."

That jolted the man to attention. "What?"

"Yes, we'll probably die in here. But if you let them kill us, you'll teach the world how evil they are."[27]

The man's spirit immediately rose with dignity and purpose.

Frankl spent time in four concentration camps, including Auschwitz, and was the only member of his family to survive. In 1945 he returned to Vienna where he wrote a book based on his observations and theories. Writing the book was a way to process, heal, and gain purpose from his wretched experience. His work started a movement called logotherapy, which encouraged people to find a redemptive perspective of their suffering.

While working with patients in a mental hospital, he became known for his success in lowering suicide rates. He would have the patients identify a project they could work on—one where someone would suffer if they didn't complete it. He didn't care what it was. It could be as simple as creating a garden that brought beauty to other patients. As he worked with them, he helped them rewrite the narrative in their head on what their life was about.

We each live by our own set of rules, beliefs, and expectations of life, but what if these aren't serving well in our quest to find purpose? Then it's time to exchange them for ones that will create a more meaningful, liberating narrative. Many research studies have revealed that in general, people with a higher sense of purpose feel more confident, have a more positive self-image and better mental health, sleep better, live longer, and transition better into adulthood.

Let's look at six common myths about purpose that might be keeping you trapped at your crossroads.

6 MYTHS ABOUT LIFE PURPOSE

Myth #1: I have to find the right destination for my life. If I miss it, I risk screwing up my entire life.

I felt the panic of believing this myth when I was twenty, and I see other high school students buckle under the belief that their university major will dictate the rest of their life. The pressure and panic return when they graduate from university and realize they need to choose their job. Because they have tied their purpose solely to their career success, they become depressed and disillusioned.

During my last months in Banff, I knew two things: my season there was over, and I wasn't ready to move back to my hometown. But where else in Canada would I go? I was still saving up to enroll in one of the courses I had set my heart on in Australia, but I wanted to settle somewhere I could come back to. Having already had two vague interactions with God on divine direction, I figured He was leaving it up to me to choose again. I eliminated the provinces that had no trees or mountains, were too isolated, required mastery of French, or didn't have promising job prospects. That pretty much left Ontario. All along I included God in the conversation, not really expecting Him to speak up. So, when one day the name "St. Catharines" imprinted in my mind, I thought that was odd. I didn't even know where it was. Maybe someone I met in Banff mentioned they were from there. I didn't give it much thought.

A week later my mom was catching me up on the news from home and mentioned that our pastor had resigned and accepted a church in St. Catharines, Ontario.

My heart thumped loudly. "What did you say?"

I grinned, feeling giddy. This was no coincidence. At that moment I realized, wherever I moved, I needed to be part of a church again. I'd had my season of restoration, and now I was ready to be part of something again. Being away from family, I would need to be part of a community that would quickly become my friends and family. Having watched my pastor walk my home church through a transformation, I knew he was embarking on a similar mission at his new church, and that was a place I could call home. I was moving to St. Catharines! All I had to do was find out where it was.

Truth #1: Though you might feel called to choose a particular path, your purpose is not defined by the destination. It's refined by a direction, expressed in how you travel and revealed as you impact others along the way.

Myth #2: My purpose earns me value and worth by doing something helpful or significant.

"I need to find my purpose. I feel like I'm dying inside, and I don't know what to do." A client sat across from me, choking out those words and looking embarrassed to be crying in a coffee shop.

I had thought we would dive into ideas for exploring a new career transition, but clearly we had some foundational work to do first. Within thirty minutes we uncovered what purpose meant to Alana and why she was so desperate for it. She realized that because of cruel, thoughtless words spoken to her, she felt as if she had no worth. To her, being able to help others gave her value as a person. However, we show up differently when we present ourselves for others to meet our needs rather than doing so because the expertise or time we have to offer is needed. We began to shift her perspective. She started recognizing that her contribution to the world was an expression of value she already had, not a reason to earn love and acceptance.

Truth #2: We had value before we ever accomplished anything. Because you were created with love, you were also given purpose. God invites you to make an impact only you can make through your approach, experience, and strengths.

Myth #3: My purpose and value depend on my success and status.

This myth wrecks us the moment failure crashes into our life. Sometimes, our failures are because we messed up and have to face the consequences. Other times, what we considered a success wasn't what others involved considered as success.

Two years and five jobs after moving to Ontario, I landed in my dream job: working in a church passionate about bringing hope to their community. I loved troubleshooting administrative challenges and developing systems, but when the novelty wore off, I felt inferior as the admin girl. What I loved about it also drove me nuts. The innovative culture kept me from getting bored, but the frequent changes frustrated me. Completing projects with excellence resonated with my sense of success, and the changes often upended what I was working on. Few people acknowledged the red flags I saw in the details or recognized my value beyond updating databases, beyond the checklist on my job description, so for years I felt overlooked.

When I chose to see my role differently, something shifted. Instead of seeing myself as the admin girl, I realized that through my position I was helping people find belonging and live up to their potential. That was my passion behind improving databases and processes. The more I believed in the bigger purpose of my role, the less I needed my value affirmed by others. As my confidence in my worth and contributions increased, I became more resilient in recovering from the blows of disappointment.

When does your sense of value come undone? Getting crickets on a social media post instead of comments? Not getting into the schools you felt led to apply for? The financial and productivity impact of a pandemic lockdown? A confrontation with your boss? An imperfect work evaluation, or a lower exam mark than you hoped for?

You know you're believing this myth when you allow disappointment and failure to cripple you.

Truth #3: Your purpose can be revealed and redefined through life's pain, failures, and disappointments.

Myth #4: Purpose is one thing for my whole life.

If believing you've been sentenced to one role or one achievement makes you bored or stressed, you're not alone. A couple years ago when I asked some entrepreneurs what myths had held them back in figuring out their path in life, this myth surfaced the most.

Selena spent eleven years as a journalist overseas. It was all she had wanted to do since she could remember. As a military kid she moved every few years, and she loved the open perspective she gained from experience in different cultures. Finding stories worth investigating took time and effort, but the rush at the end was worth it every time. She thought she had to settle on one thing as her purpose, and she was content that this was it . . . until finding love led to settling down and raising three kids. In her younger years she assumed she could only land on one thing as her purpose, and it stressed her out. Gradually she realized her purpose flourished when each role was nurtured in her life—being a mom, a storyteller, and an advocate for literacy.

Truth #4: Your purpose can be expressed in different seasons, roles, or directions in your life.

Myth #5: My purpose has to be my career.

Students aren't the only ones who limit their definition of purpose to a career. Mom guilt is the nemesis of purpose. When Lucy become a mom, she let go of the one thing she loved, teaching dance, so she could stay home with the treasure she had been praying for. After exploring several work-from-home income ideas, she realized how frustrating it was to believe her purpose had to be the thing supporting her family financially. It felt as if her passion wasn't legitimate if it wasn't her career. She found greater meaning once she started dance classes again and found another way to pay the bills.

The career quandary is stressful for many moms. One mom feels horrible for pursuing a career instead of staying home with her kids. The other stays home with her kids because she believes it's better for her family, but she secretly longs to feel alive the way she had when she was working. One homeschooling mom decides to start a business while still homeschooling, fighting the guilt of not being present for her children every moment of the day. Another finally lets go of homeschooling—something she had felt called to do for years—so she can focus on a business she loves.

Truth #5: Your purpose is more than a role or a job. It's a noun and a verb. It's about being first, then doing. Your purpose can thrive when you're fully present in each season, wherever you are.

Myth #6: I must know everything about my purpose before I take action.

If you're a detail-obsessed perfectionist like I was, you might carry this "gotta have everything just right" belief in many areas of life, from choosing a career to starting a side hustle, leading a church group, or writing a book. Perhaps you didn't start out this way, but after life's hard knocks, you've become cautious.

Many times I've looked back at points in my life and wondered, "I started out aiming for *abc* and ended up at *xyz*. How did I get here?"

In reality it's enough to know you were created to make the world a better place. Each mission might look different. Life might not turn out the way you expect, but that doesn't mean you've failed at life. Maybe you'll only see the common thread through the seasons when you look back on your life.

Truth #6: Your potential expands through five key areas: identity, skills, experiences, passions, and impact on others. Believing myths about your potential keeps you at status quo. The more action you take despite your uncertainty, the more you will discover how to make the world a better place with what you've been given.

Dare to Identify Myths You Believe

What myths are holding you back from a path of purpose? What could be possible if you didn't believe that myth? If you still find yourself stuck thinking differently, ask someone you admire what options they see could be possible.

11

READY TO BLOOM:
Principles for Thriving

"Truly charity has no limit; for the love of God has been poured into our hearts by His Spirit dwelling in each one of us, calling us to a life of devotion and inviting us to bloom in the garden where He has planted and directing us to radiate the beauty and spread the fragrance of His Providence."

—The Bishop of Geneva, Saint
Francis de Sales (1567-1622)

As I headed out my door for a brisk walk around the block, a small succulent with a splash of red caught my eye. How many times had I walked by the neighbourhood garden and never noticed it? It was no wonder. Its low-to-the-ground spread with its dense, petite, grey-green leaves was not much larger than my hand. I might not have noticed except that I had hosted a succulent mini garden workshop for women that week. The more I learned about these hearty little plants, the more I fell in love with them. The red, daisy-like flower smiled up at me as it drank in the blue sky.

The next day I noticed the little succulents again and knelt for a closer look. The red flowers had tightened into buds under the cloudy, darkened sky.

Later, as the day grew warmer and brighter, the flowers unfolded—little masterpieces ready to delight anyone who noticed their intricacy.

When I think of purpose, a verse in the Bible, Ephesians 2:10 (NIV), comes to mind: "For we are God's handiwork, created in Christ Jesus to do good works, which God prepared in advance for us to do." The administrative part of me likes that God prepared things in advance—He's not winging it. I also like the idea of being a masterpiece—a work of art He's proud of. Whether you're living at your fullest potential or hidden in winter's bleakness, waiting to blossom, He's delighted in what He's created.

On life's cloudy days, when I wasn't ready to display the beauty He created in me, I knew He saw the potential I had. I wasn't defined by that day's mood or activities.

Plants were created for a simple life: grow, bloom, reproduce. Some days, when you're restless or stressed, I'm sure you wish your life was that simple. Someone else chooses where you're planted, and you grow, bloom, and reproduce as you were made to do.

We're a little more complex than flowers. As someone who appreciates the details as well as the grand vision, biblical teaching often felt oversimplified to me. Certain verses were quoted all the time. They were the first ones I memorized as a child. They were given to me as gifts, quoted in prayers, and referred to in heartbreaking times.

One reminded me that I was special, created on purpose:

You created my inmost being; you knit me together in my mother's womb. I praise you because I am fearfully and wonderfully made; your works are wonderful, I know that full well. —Psalm 139:13-14 (NIV)

Another verse reminded me that I had a purpose:

"For I know the plans I have for you," declares the Lord, "plans to prosper you and not to harm you, plans to give you hope and a future." —Jeremiah 29:11 (NIV)

Of course when someone experienced tragedy, made a mistake, or simply had a rotten day, I could count on someone whipping out the classic spiritual band-aid:

And we know that in all things God works for the good of those who love him, who have been called according to his purpose. —Romans 8:28 (NIV)

Don't get me wrong. In that moment these gave me peace and assurance that good things were in store. If you've been around church at all, you've probably heard those verses too, maybe even clung to them as I did. But after the feel-good moments, I would wonder, *But now what? How does this verse help me figure out what to do when life doesn't turn out the way I planned?*

It wasn't until I decided to read the entire Bible chronologically in one year that I gained a clearer understanding. After years of reading my Bible almost every day and hearing sermons and lessons throughout the week, I was getting bored with it. Of course, it's not very spiritual to say something like that, so I never said it aloud. God and my faith in Him were my strength in life, and I wanted a fresh way to read the familiar words. I went to a book warehouse, and a Bible caught my eye—the *One Year Chronological Bible.*

Perfect! I thought.

I started reading it as soon as I got home and discovered that not only was each book of the Bible arranged in chronological order, but each passage had been as well. Each section had an introduction with historical context: the culture, the author, who he was writing about, and who he was writing to. Already I felt more eager to read the Bible than I had in years.

It took me eighteen months to finish.

By the end I was in awe. Those feel-good verses seemed minute compared to the magnitude of God's story—a story that arched over centuries, beyond time itself. Those verses didn't quite mean what I thought they did. They weren't meant in the way everyone quoted them.

Jeremiah 29:11 was a declaration of hope to a nation exiled to a foreign land whose way of living was in direct violation of how God had mandated His people to live. Yet they were there because after centuries of patient warnings, God finally let them experience their worst nightmare while still preserving His master plan of redemption. The "plans to prosper" were directed to a body of people united in one great story. In our individualistic Western culture, that doesn't sit very well with us. The heart of God is always the same, so I never doubted He had a hopeful future for me, but it was both sobering and reassuring to realize that everything I'm striving for isn't about me. I have a place in His grand story.

God's master plan of redemption had everything to do with Jesus. To show us at our level another way of living, God took on the form of a human. He broke rules, touched the untouchable, recruited the unqualified, and showed everyone what it looks like to live from love and wholeness rather than fear and rules. After showing us God in human likeness for thirty-three years on earth, Jesus ascended back to heavenly realms, leaving the responsibility on us to demonstrate this new way of living—and invite others into it too!

Romans 8:28 is not a spiritual band-aid that promises everything is going to be okay. The guy who wrote it was beaten, imprisoned, and misunderstood by his peers. His readers lived in a city that fed humans to lions for entertainment. They weren't into spiritual band-aids. Instead, the entire Romans 8 chapter is a promise that no matter how messy life gets, God can redeem it into something beautiful by continuing to shape us into the likeness of Jesus. It remind us of the unnegotiable power of his love, regardless of our circumstances.

How does this help you figure out what to do when you're at a crossroads? What does this have to do with narrowing down your options when you have too many ideas? How will it help you find the courage to take your next best step? When you're dragging your feet, brimming with unmotivated potential, how do you know which project to choose and which one to let go? How does it help after what you thought was a worthwhile decision leaves you feeling wrung out and lost?

The succulent can show us ways to thrive.

SUCCULENT PRINCIPLES FOR FINDING YOUR WAY

One spring, a friend and I set out on a mission to connect some busy but lonely women by planning a get-together. We decided we would make succulent mini gardens. Armed with pictures from Pinterest and boxes of supplies from a greenhouse, I was excited for us to play in some dirt, create a lovely planter, laugh, and chat.

Since I had killed my first couple of succulents, I figured if I was going to lead this workshop and deliver an inspirational talk, I'd better learn a little more about what keeps them alive. Little did I know these tiny plants offered valuable lessons for thriving through life changes.

1. You're best when you're stressed.

Most succulents start green, but as they are exposed to the sun and heat, they blush with colour. Some kinds have red-tinged leaves, and others fully turn shades of pink or purple while some will even blossom. Of course, too much sun isn't good either, but without a little stress the plant doesn't reach its full potential. We're similar. We prefer life to be in our control. But often we don't find out what we're capable of until we get uncomfortable.

2. Start with less.

My first succulent was given to me in appreciation for an act of kindness. I kept the cute white pot on my desk, admiring it and watering it faithfully—till it started getting brown and floppy. While preparing for the workshop a couple of years later, I discovered these little plants need very little water or space to thrive. In my diligent caring for my gift, I had over-watered it, causing the roots to rot. In life we thrive with less than we think we need. Often, we feel we don't have enough _____ (fill in the blank: talent, time, resources, skill, passion) to make a difference in our world. But sometimes it's the tiny micro steps that count and the constraints that cultivate creativity. Start with what you have and watch what grows.

3. Protect your bloom.

My succulent came with a whitish film on the leaves. I thought I was being helpful by wiping it off and shining the leaves. Apparently not. This frosted layer, also called "bloom," helps protect the plant from the sun, water, pathogens, and insects. As a water and insect repellent it keeps the dirt out, and as a sunscreen the waxy coating helps keep the water in, making the leaves plump and lush. This reminds me of values: they protect us from things that might compromise our purpose, focus, and energy.

4. Thrive in a tribe.

While my one little succulent shriveled away in its adorable white pot with plenty of space, the ones in my front garden seemed to crowd their way into the brick border as they multiplied. I discover that while my single plant had withered from overwatering, it also might have died of loneliness. Succulents thrive when they share space with others. Similarly, we thrive when we're in a tribe, stabilized by roots intertwined and sprouting new life. When we're left alone with our overactive thoughts, it's easy to feel like we're drying up. Find your people, and you'll thrive in your purpose.

5. Brokenness births hope.

In preparing for the gardening get-together, I came across one woman[28] who proudly cared for her young succulents until someone in her home knocked over the little pot. Dismayed, she picked up the small plant and discovered its leaves had broken off. She placed them back in the container, watering it now and then. Days later she was delighted to see little shoots stemming from the broken end of the plant, ready to take root. Our experiences are like this little plant. We can dismiss them, maybe even toss them away as useless. But often they are the beginning of a new start. It's through experiences of brokenness, disappointment and, yes, joy that we can lead others to hope and comfort.

So, we've donned a compass mindset and learned a few principles from the succulent. Next, let's see how these lessons not only help us recognize our purpose but help us continue to blossom in six key areas: our identity, experiences, delights/disturbances, tribe, skills, and values.

Dare to Believe You Can Thrive

As you embark deeper into your growth journey, which principle would you find helpful as your mantra?

- o Whether I'm living my fullest potential or waiting, hidden in winter's bleakness, God delights in me.

- o I'm best when I'm stressed. It strengthens me and reveals what I'm capable of.

- o I can start with less and watch it grow.

- o I protect my bloom with my values and priorities.

- o I thrive in a tribe.

- o My brokenness can inspire others.

BLOSSOMING IN PURPOSE

Living your purpose is more than accomplishing one mission or having perfectly aligned circumstances. A purpose filled life emerges as you blossom into the best version of you, in all seasons and areas of your life.

12

BLOSSOMING THROUGH EXPERIENCES

I found out my husband was leaving me on my lunch break. The guy from Banff and I had kept up a long-distance relationship, which led to him following me out to Ontario where we got married. Three and a half years later I was sick of us both walking on eggshells. I was fatigued from steeling myself against moody reactions and wondering what I did wrong. I was tired of being broke while we both tried out jobs we hoped we would find fulfilling.

A couple weeks prior he announced he wanted to go camping in Algonquin Park. I perked up. We had been wanting to go for a while—I heard the canoeing in the lakes surrounded by northern woods would be beautifully serene. It would be a scramble, but I figured I could arrange for last-minute time off work, so I said, "Ok, let's go."

He looked apologetic but firm. "I mean, I'm going to go by myself. I just need to get away alone."

Bracing my heart, I thought, *I can be understanding instead of taking it personally. If this is what he needs to get out of this funk, I'm up for anything.*

My birthday came around a few days after he came back. I was hoping we'd have some kind of connection moment with him acknowledging it—and me. After all, he'd had enough time and solitude away to come back refreshed. Instead, he barely looked at me as he said, "I didn't think we could afford anything, so I didn't get you a present or a card."

Oh.

By the end of the next week, I'd had enough. No more avoiding conflict and squirmy conversations. No more tiptoeing on eggshells. This was no way to live life. I came home on my lunch break to him watching TV and said, "I need to know what's going on. Can we please talk? Whatever you're dealing with, I want us to be partners in whatever we're facing. Just start somewhere. I don't want you to be scared of telling me stuff." I was desperate to bridge the gap and make him see that I wanted to be approachable in this. So, I pulled out the first example I could think of.

"Tell me anything—even if it's that you don't love me."

He muted the TV, shifted uncomfortably, and sat silently for long heartbeats.

"I've been gathering the courage to tell you . . ."

My stomach felt queasy.

"I don't love you anymore."

I felt slammed. Stunned. Then I wanted to throw up. My brain started to cloud, and I tried to make sense of what he was saying.

"I don't know if I ever loved you . . . I married you for the wrong reasons—'cause I was scared of being lonely. It's why I pressured you to rush the wedding. All this time I've been feeling guilty, and it's making me feel anxious about everything. I don't want you to think I don't care about you. I do. I don't want to hurt you, but I don't want to live this life, live with your high expectations . . . I need to find myself again. I don't want this marriage anymore."

Then my lunch break was over.

No one prepared me to handle a moment like this. I had committed to lifelong marriage—to making it work, even if times got hard. I didn't know what else to do, what else to say, so I went back to work where at least I knew I was loved and appreciated. I hadn't expected life would be a fairy tale, but what did this mean?

Three days later he moved away, and I was left to figure out how to deal with my shock, pain, questions. At what point had things gone wrong? I had no idea. Had it been the day our relationship shifted from friendship to dating? Or the moment I agreed to a short engagement? The times I gave him support and grace to find what he wanted to do with his life? Were my expectations really too high? I loved him, but had I misjudged him that badly and married the wrong guy?

Living through grief, loss, and rejection is a tumultuous paradox of emotions. It's hard to think straight. I would feel numb, I would even smile, and then break down into tears the next moment—which was a little awkward for guests standing across the reception desk at work. Funny how you can feel fine and not fine all at the same time.

I had more support from my friends and colleagues than I could have imagined, but everything changed. My view of life was now tinged with pain.

The first Sunday, I walked into my church and hid in the dark back corner, needing to be around people but not wanting to talk to anyone. As soon as I realized the message was on marriage, I nearly bolted. But I forced myself to stay, achy heart and all, determined not to run from this. In my job, part of my role was to be the first point of contact for engaged couples who wanted to plan their wedding with a pastor. I would feel happy for them but also sad, knowing they blissfully had no idea of the trouble they would face one day. Usually, if anyone in authority or with a stronger opinion questioned me, I would back down and second-guess myself. At least now I had the confidence to stand my ground when couples wanted to rush a wedding or skip premarital counselling. Friendships drifted apart, either because the memories were too hard or because it was too hard to relate the way we used to.

Over the first months, well-meaning people stopped me to offer their sympathies. Some wanted to confront him and convince him to come back. Others thought they were showing support with snide remarks about him. A few thought it would be helpful to tell me he wasn't good enough for me and that they knew the marriage wouldn't last. That only made me mad. One man told me my ex reminded him of what it was like when he married his wife, but she eventually came around, and they had a thriving family now. I needed that reassurance because most people's comments had me questioning my discernment when I thought I had gotten married with my eyes open.

WHEN LIFE FALLS APART

What do you do when your life and dreams fall apart? What do you decide at a crossroads when the bridge you wanted to cross has collapsed? How do you choose where to go when the paths available to you were never ones you planned on travelling?

An ordinary lunch break turns life upside down. An everyday drive to a meeting turns into months of recovery in the hospital and accumulating bills. The business you thought was successful is going under because you didn't hire the person you thought you hired. You turn forty, and you grapple with the realization that life hasn't turned out the way you expected.

I'm so grateful for the grace and support I received in those years of recovery from my separation. No one could show me the exact path of reconciliation I wanted nor how to handle my internal roller coaster. People offered suggestions and wisdom, but no one understood enough to help me figure out my life choices. So, God was my guide. I was left to face the unhealthy patterns I was starting to see in myself. I needed

His comfort, strength, and guidance hour by hour, sometimes minute by minute. As I leaned into the pain, determined to find healing and make this a redemptive story, I slowly saw how God was giving me a new sense of purpose.

Soon I found myself co-leading a small group of people wrestling with their own pain, questions, and disappointments. Even when I felt too bleak to inspire any of them, I knew this was where I needed to be. Because of my rejection I saw and understood the pain of a whole new demographic of people. I had a more profound acceptance of a gray world where things weren't as black and white as I thought they were. I had much more grace and love for others who hadn't made the wisest choices in life.

No experience is wasted.

Whether it's a failure, a loss, or a tragedy, your experience becomes not only part of who you are but part of what impassions your purpose. The best part of it is that you get to choose what the experience means in the story you're living. It might hurt like hell. But you still get to choose whether you'll be the helpless victim or the main character embarking on their hero's journey.

Your past experiences can prepare you for your present crossroads. The good news is that whatever path you choose, whatever you encounter on the other side, this too will be something that positions you for the next thing.

Dare to Blossom Through Your Experiences

Think of a time you experienced a challenge or setback. What did you learn through it? How did you become better through it? How might you have missed an opportunity to blossom through it?

13

BLOSSOMING IN YOUR IDENTITY

Leah was a spunky, fun girl to hang out with at one of my jobs years ago. Once, she dropped a cup and with a little laugh told me her family called her Klutz because she was always clumsy. At first, it sounded like a passing comment. When I caught the resignation in her voice and the pain in her eyes, I realized those words had shaped her perception of herself (and maybe even made her more prone to clumsiness). It was beginning to form the story she believed about herself.

How do you describe who you are?

Labels

Labels describe who we are but are often negative names that stuck from our past stories. We get in trouble when we let names constrain us instead of revealing who we truly are. We might have only one given name, but our identity can be cluttered with pseudonyms.

Bully. Wimp. High achiever. Slowpoke. Stupid good-for-nothing. Mine were Bossy, Churchy, and Perfectionist. Labels aren't your true self. They are what you conformed to because at the time you didn't know any other way to cope.

Positions or titles
Positions or titles define the status or rank you hold within an organization or unit.

Whenever I had to check off my marital status on a form, I felt angry and nauseous. For four years I couldn't even check off "divorced," which felt loathsome enough. Instead, I was separated—a marital status option only provided on some forms. Trouble arises when you think a position sums up all you are. At my current job I have held five different titles. By the time I was given the third one, I realized they don't define me. That realization was freeing.

Roles
Roles define how you perform what you do.

In the first year of my marriage separation, I realized I was still living as a rescuer. If I didn't address my core needs and reestablish healthy boundaries, I would continue to attract the kind of friends who needed rescuing. Yet, a positive role I held was that of big sister. Even though I had moved far from my siblings, I often found myself gravitating to students ten years younger than I as an encourager, den mom, or roommate.

You might be the peacemaker or the clown in your family. In your business you might hold the title of CEO, but maybe you're performing the roles of marketer and bookkeeper too. The roles you hold can be necessary but turn unhealthy when carried beyond their season.

Affinity descriptors
These names signify when we've owned a skill or interest as part of who we are, for better or worse.

We all have natural gifts and inclinations, whether innate or nurtured. When we move from calling ourselves "someone who likes coffee" to "a coffee specialist," it carries a deeper sense of identity. Identifying by a descriptor might show up innocently if you're a dog lover. But what about when you're considering your vocation? If you love streamlining processes to help small business function more efficiently, you might love being referred to as the "systems gal." However, if you are bored with systems and would rather focus on leadership development, being called the systems gal would feel more like a frustrating life sentence.

My fondness for writing books ebbed and flowed throughout seasons of my life over thirty years. Whether my knack for words or my passion drew attention, I had numerous people ask me to edit their articles and books. Depending on the season, I would call myself *someone who loves to write* or a *writer*. Then, years later I finally called myself an *author*. I felt a significant shift in ownership with each change in descriptor.

Some of your natural interests and talents last a lifetime while others are only part of your life for a season. Grieving them might make room for a descriptor that expands your identity.

Personality

Personality types provide language to describe our unique combinations of motivators, behaviours, and patterns of thinking.

As I leaned into my pain that first year of separation, I read dozens of nonfiction books on marriage, healing, and personal growth. After a personality assessment told me I was a Type 1, the Reformer, I bought this massive book called *The Wisdom of the Enneagram* to find out what that meant. I laughed and cried as I read through it. Here was something that described exactly how I viewed life and why I did what I did. I felt fully understood for the first time. Then, I came across a chart of what the Type 1 personality looked like on a spectrum from unhealthy to average to healthy. It was sobering to see I landed on the unhealthy side. Had this been presented as wrong or right, it would have triggered me to shut down because I didn't know how to be any other way.

Instead, it illuminated hope that there was a way for me to become unapologetic and confident.

> You will have to choose again and again who you want to be in your story.

There are copious personality typing tools out there. You can let them box you into expectations or use them to learn ways to thrive in your work, relationships, and life.

Character strengths

These traits are the stuff you're made of and how you handle life's responsibilities and unexpected situations when you're at your best.

When I looked back on the words my classmates used to describe me in their notes—words such as *servant-heartedness, honesty, wisdom*—I realized they were referring to my character strengths. Sometimes called *values*, these are qualities that help you meet the demands of life. After my marriage broke down, I knew the following season of healing would test my character like never before. It would have been natural to hold onto hurt and resentment. Instead, I resolved to be open to trust again. I chose to be humble enough to own my growth. I decided to be gracious. It was dang hard.

You too will have to choose again and again who you want to be. What character strengths will you need to lean on to become that person?

Belonging

Where do "they" end and "I" begin? What part do I have in this bigger story? I found myself asking these kinds of questions as a young adult exploring my role in my family. They came up in marriage as I tried to figure out how to be my own person and yet still "be one" with my husband. These questions arose when loyalty to my employer's expectations enveloped my life. Navigating singlehood far from my family, I grappled with these questions at Christmas when all my friends had family gatherings to attend. It arose at weddings when everyone else had a date. It surfaced when I was the only one who hadn't seen the movie everyone else was quoting or in discussions on beliefs I didn't share.

Studies have shown that your relationships contribute to the development of your identity. Belonging helps reinforce your core identity. It can also mask it if you believe the illusion of fitting in rather than belonging as you are.

As Brené Brown says, "True belonging doesn't require you to change who you are; it requires you to be who you are."[29] To be who you are, you need to *know* who you are.

Is how you define yourself truly who you are? It might. But it doesn't have to be. If those names and descriptors aren't reflective of the character you want to become in your story, it's time to blossom.

Dare to Blossom in Your Identity

What are some words you and others use to describe who you are? How are these helping you at this crossroads? How are they hindering you?

14

BLOSSOMING WITH DELIGHTS
AND DISTURBANCES

I had gone through a lot of healing and growing, and I figured out my new normal over the next few years after my husband left. The small group of peers I co-led had doubled and split into two groups. I was now leading one in my apartment. One night like any other, the conversation grew more intense as one woman shared her struggle. Another person offered insight. Another empathized and shared her own plight. It was a normal group night, and I felt alive being a part of it.

Here I was, connecting people, creating a safe environment for them to share, and guiding conversation where it needed to go, but this was so much more. It was part of the journey of transformation and belonging.

The thought sparked a flashback to that desperate moment in my bunk in Guatemala a decade earlier when I asked God, "What do you want me to do with my life?" and I received the dreaded quiet response, "Go back to Canada and impact your generation."

This is what I was born to do. I felt the euphoric chills of a time-stands-still moment.

Finally, I knew. *This is it! This is what you meant, God. And. I. Love. It!*

Passion is the fuel that drives you forward, and it's the contagious energy that inspires others. It's a directional desire that might start as an interest and turn into growing curiosity. When full throttle, it refuses to be ignored. You won't always have seasons where you're doing what you love. Yes, there are seasons where you're miserable at work, yet you don't feel free to follow your passion. There are times when you feel as if you are in limbo, waiting for one path to end and the next one to begin, but that's a great time to take inventory.

What keeps you up at night or makes you cry? What gets you talking when otherwise you would stay quiet? What makes you lose all track of time? When did you last laugh so hard you peed your pants? Living by "should's" usually requires gritted teeth, fake smiles, and deep breaths. Living by what delights and disturbs you squishes hours into minutes, makes you smile, and spurs you to action. This is worth considering at your crossroads.

If the word passion feels too intense to, think back to the levels of intensity mentioned in chapter eight around directional desires.

At first, things that delight and disturb you catch your attention. When interest turns into curiosity, you begin to explore them or rally against them. Over time you begin recognizing patterns beyond a single event or environment. Maybe you've always dreamed of writing a book but spent most of your life dismissing the idea as unattainable—until one year when you realize the dream has never gone away, and maybe it's worth investing in. Your heart leaps the moment you actually give it consideration, and suddenly you realize you can't *not* write the book. Or perhaps you're embarrassed to admit you've held twenty-three jobs in your life. But as you look back on what bothered you about each one enough to quit, you realize you've learned a lot about organizational systems that work. You also thrive at starting new things and making them better, but if there's no room for your ideas, you move on. This revelation propels you to start your own business as a consultant.

As you pay attention to what consistently draws you, one day you'll have the confidence to announce, "This is my passion—and I'm going all in!"

The annoying and inspiring thing about blossoming through your passion is that you expect everyone else to get fired up about it too. But is your fervor meant to be adopted by everyone? There's more to a dream than merely pursuing a passion.

Dare to Blossom with Your Passions

What kinds of issues, interests, or big questions keep you up at night? What makes you cry? What gets you talking when otherwise you would stay quiet? What makes you smile or feel alive inside?

15

BLOSSOMING WITH YOUR TRIBE

That euphoric moment when I connected the dots to *this is what I was meant for* was exactly that—a moment. It held relief. Delight. Excitement.

And then it was gone.

It wasn't a life plan. It was a confirmation that I was in the right place at the right time, doing something that made me feel alive. I had been doing it for a couple years though. Why had that moment stood out to me? Maybe it's because this time I wasn't the helper, the co-leader, or the person in someone else's space. I was leading on my own in my apartment. Or maybe it's because I was trusting God's Spirit and my intuition to facilitate what these friends needed in their spiritual journeys.

Still, restlessness had started to mingle with the delight of that epiphany. The conversations started sounding the same.

One day, I pulled a copy of *The On-Purpose Person* by Kevin McCarthy off my bookshelf. The book had led me to some of my *aha* moments over the previous decade. If the book had such a clarifying impact in my life, of course everyone else would love it . . . wouldn't they? Reading a book. Homework. Self-assessments and reflection exercises. What's not to love?

In our next meeting, before we dove into the final session of our series, I announced this was the book study we would begin the following week.

We started our book study the next meeting, and a few meetings and chapters later, group members got "busier" and faded away. A couple women stayed around for the conversation but looked bored. Their conversations trailed off to catty fights at work, passive boyfriends, and renovations. Their issues seemed suddenly meaningless to me. They showed no interest in looking at the patterns in their life that hinted at what they were created for. That change puzzled me.

Halfway through the book the group had shrunk down to half. These were the men and women whose curiosity grew with each chapter we discussed. How would they be able to define their life purpose by the end of our study?

I spent hours during the week creating exercises to help the group articulate their mission statements, uncover their core values, and identify their defining life moments. Like the giddy writing nerd I was, I brought dictionaries and thesauruses to help us craft our statements. The men and women poured over them with as much intrigue as I had hoped they would.

In our last meeting together, each person wrote a statement they felt reflected their life's purpose. These weren't declarations they wanted to shout from rooftops. They were pliable statements that gave fresh meaning to their past challenges and future desires. It was something they would take with them in life as new seasons unfolded.

As each one read aloud their purpose statement, I beamed. Though some still felt their statements were inadequate reflections of their heart, they were each proud of what they had crafted and the journey that led them there. We shared a bond at that moment, having experienced something others abandoned.

Eventually, the group disbanded, but this clarity emerged: not everyone wanted to think about or own their purpose beyond everyday existence, and I wanted to invest my time in people who did.

Is it okay to define the kind of people I want to inspire? I wondered.

Should we only ever spend time with people who enjoy the same things we do? We blossom when first we see the opportunities to add value to, glean from, and connect with the people already in our lives. People's attitudes, viewpoints, and habits are contagious. The more aware we are of how we're affected by those around us or how we're affecting them, the better we can shape the person we want to become.

At a crossroads you realize you need to be more intentional about the people you give your time and attention. Whether it's the stage of life your family is in, the type of clients you want to help, or who you go for coffee with, at some point you'll need to choose one person over another. When you don't have clarity about who you are committed to serving, it will play tug of war on your time, heart, and energy. Saying yes to everyone means spreading yourself thin, and no one actually gets the best you. Saying no with purpose, though you might feel like you're letting someone down, actually releases you to blossom.

It took me years to admit it aloud, but I was drawn to connect with people hungry for the discovery of who they were meant to be. I wanted to help them believe in themselves and make the most of their part in a greater story.

I knew the who . . . but now what?

Dare to Blossom with Your Tribe

What kind of people do you tend to avoid? What is it about them (or you) that triggers that response? Is this something you need to lean away from or lean towards?

What kind of people do you have a soft spot for? What have they experienced? What are they feeling?

16

BLOSSOMING IN YOUR SKILLS

The fifth part of your life you get to see blossom is your skills. It might involve gifts and abilities you already have. Or it might require developing new skills. When we're facing a crossroads, brand new paths can be exciting or daunting. Sometimes without fully realizing it, we narrow our options because we feel we must make a choice based on what we know how to do.

"I'm not a very good at _____, so I could never _____."

"I don't know how to _____, so I can't _____."

"I'm a _____, so _____ happens to me."

When we treat our abilities as a life sentence, we'll live out a self-fulfilling prophecy. But when we acknowledge the skills as avenues for expansion and impact, our opportunities multiply.

During that season of leading my small group to finding their purpose, my restlessness grew dark and despondent. I was four years into a divorce, bored with my work, and stuck in writer's block. It was frustrating.

One day, I was in a team development retreat in a room of pastors, leaders, and support staff seated around tables. Drifting off to look at Lake Ontario stretching across the grey horizon, I could see the faint skyline of Toronto and the point of the CN Tower. Mark Collins, the consultant leading the session at the front of the room, called on me to demonstrate goal-setting skills. Usually, being the group guinea pig would have had me squirming, but Mark and I had been swapping stories and inside jokes for years. I trusted him to not make a fool out of me.

"Emily, what's a dream you're stuck on these days?" he asked.

"Writing my novel," I answered, not quite sure what kind of answer he was looking for.

"Tell me more about this novel and the dream," he prompted.

"It's about a young adult who feels her life is falling apart and finds herself hunting down local treasure to stabilize her life again. I've been working on it off and on since I was thirteen. I always dreamed I would write this series and get it published."

The usually chatty group quieted, and he took a few steps closer. "What's behind that desire to publish your book?"

I'd never thought about my writing that way before. "That transition from teenager to adulthood can be scary and confusing. My novel would give young adults a place to escape but also feel someone identifies with them. That boost would set them up to keep figuring out life another day."

It was a mountaintop moment. The spark of clarity. Someone was curious enough to ask beyond surface questions. Someone was holding a space for me, truly listening to me instead of talking over me or thinking of their own response. It was powerful enough to tap into the confidence and motivation lying under my cluttered heart and mind.

He asked a couple more questions, and I figured out what I could do to press through my writer's block and when I would take those steps. As he entered the date I mentioned into his calendar so he could follow up, I felt honoured.

Then, Mark called on someone else who was willing to share a dream that could be achievable but seemed improbable. I watched the same process unfold. He never gave advice, fixed anything, or showed him a direction. With a few questions he unlocked a dream none of us had known about our colleague, tapped into the core desire, and uncovered the possibilities. The room was spellbound and the air thick with emotion and wonder.

I want to do that.

It wasn't a thought so much as resolve. I knew what I wanted now. This was the kind of passion and clarity I had been looking for when I was twenty, wondering how to choose a career or education path.

And now I had two learning paths to lean into: coaching skills and writing skills.

The biggest thing holding us back from becoming a master of what we love is fear.

We fear we won't be as good as we want to be. We fear missing out, so we fill our time with a bunch of little things only to realize a decade later we missed out on what we really wanted. Some of us might fear investing time and resources into developing a skill only to find out it wasn't useful at all, so we don't even start.

Blossoming in your skills can help you move on from your crossroads in two ways. The first is to get clear on a destination to aim for and to find out which skills would be most helpful along the way. The second is to follow your curiosity: keep learning all you can and see where it leads.

Because I talked about writing a book and lit up eagerly whenever someone spoke about articles or books they were writing, people would send me their work to edit. I complied because it was fun, and they trusted me even though I hadn't taken any official courses on it. My passion for writing prompted fascinating Starbucks conversations with strangers and book-editing offers I would never have thought of pursuing.

As I went through training, I didn't have a vision of a new career in coaching. I didn't know what people did with that sort of coaching skill. I only knew I wanted to get better at it, and I practiced on anyone who came to me with a problem—much to their exasperation. My vision for my life unfolded over the next years as my confidence and experience blossomed.

Whatever path you choose, the knowledge and skills you gain can be used in some way to build relationships. God can redeem anything you throw at Him and include it in His story. If you're feeling like you missed opportunities, that you're too old to go back to school or start something new . . . if you spent too many years spinning your wheels and waiting for a break, the time to step into your dream is now. Learn something new. Work with what you have or invest in something that intrigues you. Try many things or pour yourself into learning one thing stupendously well.

Doubt will creep in. Life will interfere at times, whether that means distractions, financial obligations, or health detours. Yet, in each of these situations you can learn skills and disciplines that can serve as steppingstones. They might not make sense now, but each one can offer something valuable for the next season.

Dare to Blossom in Your Skills

Often, we overlook the aptitude we have because our talents feel too natural and normal to us. Here's a skills development plan you might find helpful at your crossroads.

1. **Inventory**—What are you good at? What natural or acquired skills do you already have? What skills does your current situation require?

2. **Awareness**—How did you develop the skills you already have?

3. **Projection**—What kind of tangible and intangible skills does your dream require? What would you love to be great at if you could?

4. **Target**—What are the top two tangible, hands-on skills you need to develop this season?

5. **Optimize**—What are ways you can learn or excel at these core skills?

6. **Act**—What's your first step to action and practice in developing your key skill?

WHAT'S THE BIG DEAL?

Why does it matter to know your purpose at your crossroads? How does it help you blossom or choose your path, knowing you aren't confined to right or wrong answers?

Knowing you have options to help you evolve can be encouraging. However, if you have too many paths to consider, you might need to create some space to identify the route that aligns most with what inspires and motivates you. If you're not a fan of any of the options available to you right now, you can download the Blossoming in Purpose guide at https://daretodecide.ca/blossomguide. The exercise in it can help you look for ways your current situation can align with your sense of purpose so you can flourish.

17

BLOSSOMING WITHIN YOUR VALUES:
Protect What's Important

*"I can't tell you how many times a week I'm asked,
'How do you do it all?' My answer is, 'I don't.'"*

—Tricia Goyer, *Balanced: Finding
Center as a Work-at-Home Mom*

On the dashboard of my life, I was starting every day with my gas gauge on half full. By the end of the day, the warning light flashed its signal that I was heading toward burnout.

My novel was suffering too, but at least I knew why: I had too many characters.

Unable to keep track of who was who and why they mattered to the story, my writers' critique group told me I needed to merge and eliminate characters. After years plotting out my series, I adored all my characters. Each one was important and alive in my mind, and the thought of getting rid of one felt appalling.

Kind of like my life, I mused. *It's one thing to cut characters that don't add much to the story; but how do you do that in real life?*

Somehow, I had gone from an introvert with a couple of close friends to a life convoluted by coffee dates, relationship drama, helping friends, and Friday night hangout invitations, not to mention wrangling the three-hour time zone difference between my family and myself. I didn't even have time to date—not that I wanted to. I was dreadful at it and was quite content to rationalize my decision not to date with the reason that my divorce wasn't finalized.

The same interactions that had once made me feel alive and purposeful now stirred an inner war between my needs and others' expectations. I knew I had to figure out how to decline invitations and reprioritize how I spent my time, but I felt stuck. Telling people I couldn't hang out caused me stress, knowing I'd eventually have to fit them in, and the thought of disappointing or offending someone felt exhausting.

One night over dinner with a friend, I blurted out, "I have too many people in my life. I don't know what to do."

"Oh, I can help you with that," she said. "I've been dealing with that my whole life."

After dinner we headed to her house.

She had me write down all the people I would want to spend time with. Then she went through her calendar book and explained how she defined her relationships with the people in her life. For each category she had assigned how often she would get together with them: once a year, once a quarter, once a month, and weekly. Once she determined how often she would reach out to each person, she entered their names in her day planner as a reminder to reach out to them to set a time to get together. With this system she was able to be intentional with relationships she valued and wanted to nurture.

This sounded familiar. Mark Collins, the same consultant who introduced me to the power of curiosity in goal setting, had also taught me how to define what I wanted from the various relationships in my life. During a season when my private world was being invaded by so many people and their questions, it was a relief to know there were levels of intimacy. This knowledge helped me release guilt in many of my relationships, but I had never dared to write out specific names.

When I got home, I pulled out my notes from Mark's teaching and from what my friend had just shown me and compiled them into a chart.

In the first column I wrote out the list of all the people in my life. In the second column I made a list of my relationship categories on a broad scale.

- Acquaintances

- Casual Friends

- Close Friends

- Confidants

- Partner (I thought I may as well designate that space for whenever I did get married again.)

I added a third column to note what I valued in and/or gave to each relationship. That column represented a minus or a plus for me, giving me space to identify what aspects of this relationship drained and/or energized me.

Part of the tension with others was that we had different expectations for the relationship, whether it was the level of transparency or the amount of time they wanted to spend together. So, in the fourth column I wrote down which level of relationship I sensed they wanted from me. Acknowledging differences in our desires helped me recognize if I needed to accept the discrepancy or arrange a heart-to-heart conversation with them. The thought of confrontation terrified me, but writing it down helped me face it.

In the fifth column I wrote down how often I would want to spend time with them: annually, quarterly, monthly, weekly, or daily.

See the Relationship Chart illustration for what my chart looked like with examples of fictional people.

Relationships Chart

Name	Carson	Jen	Tara
Where do they fit in my relationship circle?	Casual Friend / History	Close Friend	Casual Friend
What do I value in the relationship? What about it energizes and/or drains me?	• Friendship was built over some work collaboration and projects. (+) • We relate to single life. (+) • Our values and shared interests have changed.(-)	• Listens well, understanding. (+) • Helps people by nailing the main issue and helping them own—inspiring (+) • We share leadership in some areas.(+) • Conflicted by demands at home with her family and our commitments. (-)	• Always seems burdened.(-) • Enjoys spending time with me, and I don't mind helping her if she wants to grow, but it doesn't energize me.(-)

Where do I probably fit into their relationships circle?	The season is shifting. Used to be a casual confident. Now we gravitate to other people, have less in common. I'm probably a casual friend now.	She sees me more as a close friend/confidant, but she's been hanging out with some other people.	She keeps asking to go for coffee. Seems to think I'm a close friend/confidant.
Time: How often do I want to spend time with this person? In what context? What does this relationship's level require of me?	None. We used to hang out once a week. Now I'm okay with not spending time together anymore.	Before—we used to talk/text 2-4x a week for 2 hrs. Now—2x week, no more than an hour Sundays or Mondays.	Before—2x month Now—one coffee every two months on Mondays or Tuesdays

Yep, I could see why my friend never told people she did this. It could easily hurt feelings and cause misunderstandings. It felt weird to write all that down. But by not defining the gap between my needs and expectations and theirs, our feelings were being hurt anyway. Without addressing this, either I would become reclusive and empty, or my stress would lead to burnout.

As I looked over my chart, more clarity came to me.

KNOW YOUR CORE VALUES

We all have conscious and unconscious beliefs by which we live. Ways we respond to others. What we expect from others. How we show up for the commitments and activities that matter to us. Behind each of these rules is a value.

Values are what's important to you. Because they're part of who you are, shaped by your experiences, there's no need to justify them. They aren't right or wrong—they simply are. That's why they're at the centre of you blossoming.

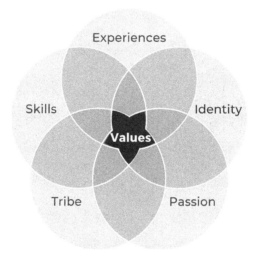

If you were to list the experiences that impacted you negatively or positively, you would be able to extract a value from each story. Think about a moment when you felt delighted. What did you enjoy about it? What part made you feel happy? At the heart of the experience, you probably felt connected with something you valued. What was it?

Now, reflect on a time you felt disturbed about something. What about that situation made you the most angry or uncomfortable? Dig a little deeper into that thought. What was at stake in that moment? What was threatened or compromised? It was probably related to something you value.

As I looked over my chart, I thought about the situations where I felt conflicted. There were the times where I felt torn between spending time with two people. While I enjoyed the thought-provoking conversation I had with one person, the other person was part of a team I was on, and maintaining our relationship set us up for success in our project. Then there was the tension I felt when I wanted to spend time writing but had committed to helping out with a local event for singles. I began to recognize some of my values: responsibility, being servant-hearted, inspiring others to be their best.

Identifying individual words was helpful, but it wasn't enough. The words could mean something different to anyone. I had to define what they meant to me:

- **Responsibility**—following through on my commitments was important to me.

- **Servant-heartedness**—leading by helping others so they can do what they feel called to do.

- **Inspiring worth**—giving people my time, attention, and encouragement so they know they are valuable and then thrive in their potential.

On their own they sounded like worthwhile values. What was causing them to collide with one another? I had to peel back another layer to discover where my tension lay.

Without defining the boundaries of my responsibilities, I had no filter for my decision-making other than whether I felt like it or not. This led me to become over-responsible.

I genuinely loved helping people, whether that meant stacking chairs after an event, helping someone move, or listening to a friend's heartbreak. But when I overcommitted, this collided with my responsibility value. I wouldn't say no, and I would find myself back into the red zone of exhaustion and resentment.

In making sure people knew they mattered, I could easily fall into the inverse of inspiring worth, believing that if I didn't give people my time and encouragement, they wouldn't know they're valuable. I knew their confidence in their worth didn't depend on my expressing it. And I also saw that if I didn't take time to rejuvenate, I wouldn't have any value to offer at all.

This collision of values went beyond my relationships. I saw a lack of balance in my work life as well. Looking back on the last few years, I recognized predictable patterns of exhaustion, pulling back, and renewal.

So, what if I was more intentional with how I managed my busy season? I mused.

PRIORITIZE WHAT MATTERS TO YOU

Creating an ideal schedule helped me figure out how to live out my values. In the past I had created my ideal week to include categories in my life such as work, relationships, impact, recreation, and personal development. This time, my preferred week focused on the types of relationships that were important to me and balanced giving and receiving dynamics in the time I set aside for them.

- God—this was already part of my morning routine (quiet time before I got ready, which includes reading my Bible, journaling, or going for a walk)

- Myself (alone time, writing, reading, turning off my brain over NCIS, cleaning, or cooking for the week)

- Others

  o Casual friends I go for coffee with or chat with in passing but don't expect anything in return

  o Close friends and confidants—people with whom I can simply be myself and who would remind me how to have fun

o Writing critique group, who inspire my writing ambitions through their accountability and colourful perspectives

o Mentors who encourage me and teach me new ways of dealing with life

o Small group time (this energizes me as long as it is once a week with meaningful conversation)

o Large groups and social gatherings (these drain me the most, but if I have a set focus in going, I feel more comfortable)

o Family (mostly long-distance calls and annual trips across the country)

Once I mapped out my ideal schedule, each relationship was given a time and frequency by week, month, quarter, or year. Investing one on one in peers a couple times a week helped me feel aligned with my purpose. Less than that and I felt bored. More than that and I felt stressed and off balance. I simply didn't want to do it at the end of the week when I had nothing left to give and needed fun and rejuvenation. Relief— or maybe it was peace—washed over me when I decided I would only reserve Friday nights for what I considered fun, whether alone or with close friends.

Because parties and events drained me and didn't offer the quality of conversations I valued, I decided invitations to these were an automatic "no, thank you" beyond once a month. I had watched others flatly turn down invitations without justifying or apologizing, and I admired that. It inspired me to give myself permission to handle these kinds of interactions with grace and confidence and not feel I had to defend, justify, or apologize for declining an invitation.

This exercise of defining and organizing what mattered to me also revealed gaps. I realized I needed to be more intentional in being around people who could speak into my life or mentor me in areas I wanted to grow.

FROM IDEAL TO REALITY

Ideal week schedules had never lasted long for me before. They were always connected to a task or a goal. No sooner did the goal lose its meaning or life unfolded differently than I intended, and I had to exchange the ideal for reality.

This time was different.

Where my previous ideal weekly plans were based on getting things done, this ideal schedule was based on my values and purpose. Life wasn't maximizing what I got done—that only made me feel like a machine. Rather, this ideal schedule helped me become the version of myself I liked, balancing what was meaningful to me.

The more I tuned into what energized and depleted me, the more I could schedule my rhythms in advance. It worked out so well that I decided to try a new approach to the most stressful season of the year. Working in a church, the month of September was chaotic with every group, program, and initiative launching all at once. Thinking through the little things others overlooked and managing increased volume of administration took over my brain and life. In previous years I would find myself crashing by mid-October with a nasty cold.

What would it take for me to not get sick in October this year? I wondered.

I pulled back on my social interactions for the month and warned them that they wouldn't see me much in September. Before the stress set in, I adjusted my meals and water intake, and I made sure I went for walks in the morning.

I set aside some restorative alone time for a few weeks. Sometimes that meant crashing in front of my favourite TV series to interrupt my brain's churning. Other times I merely enjoyed cleaning or *being*—not committing to do, organize, or solve anything but doing what felt inspiring in the moment. I also scheduled a couple days off in mid-October that I could look forward to.

When the end of October came around, I realized I hadn't been sick and didn't feel like crashing. It would be easy to slip into overtime because I had grown accustomed to it, so I put my ideal schedule back in place and made sure I was enjoying life in little ways.

I felt so empowered, seeing I could live intentionally, knowing my limits and how to make the most of my capacity.

Over the years, commitments shifted. People entered in and drifted out of the different circles of my life. The self-awareness I gleaned from that exercise in understanding my rhythms was foundational in adjusting to major changes, whether recovering from a ruptured appendix, making room for dating, or adjusting to being married again.

Those transitions were still stressful, but now I knew how to manage them more easily.

A few years ago I was on maternity leave, dreaming of what I wanted life to look like in the future. I wondered what it might look like to live from principles and values in other contexts.

I came across a woman's story that inspired me. This bestselling author of over seventy books had to figure out how to balance her family life in the midst of writing, speaking, adopting children, homeschooling, and volunteering at the local teen pregnancy center.

HOW VALUES AND PRINCIPLES HELPED TRICIA'S FAMILY

Tricia Goyer's husband John came home from work one day to find his wife crying in the kitchen, surrounded by bags of groceries. Dinner hadn't been started yet. Their kids were fighting and shrieking, and Tricia had reached a breaking point.

"I . . . can't . . . do . . . it . . . anymore," she said, sobbing.

In her early days as a stay-at-home mom, Tricia spent her morning homeschooling her kids and her afternoon writing articles for magazines. As guilty as she felt for investing in her writing dream, having publishing opportunities felt like redemption for the poor choices that had led to her to becoming a teen mom without a college degree. She felt like she was the worst homeschooling mom on the planet. Other moms seemed to be content to bake with their kids, stroll to the park, and prepare organic meals. Instead, she sent her kids to watch Barney while she got in a couple hours of writing, trying not to get cranky when they interrupted her every ten minutes for a snack or asked her to play with them. To compensate for the guilt, she poured even more energy into her parenting. Library trips. Dance lessons. Soccer. It started to feel like they spent more time in the car shuttling kids from one thing to the next than at home.

A meltdown from one of her kids was her undoing when John found them.

He wrapped her in a hug. "You don't have to do all this."

After the chaos calmed, dinner was made, and the kids were in bed, they sat down to sort out their priorities. Looking at family as a core value, they started out with a few questions:

What do we want to achieve as a family?

What will matter five years from now—ten years from now?

What will mold our children into God-serving adults?

What will bring peace—not stress—to our home?

As they talked it out, they stayed away from vague ideals such as "raising godly kids." What they needed was a practical list that would bring clarity when they would say yes or no to opportunities that came up. They needed principles that guided what ended up on their calendar and gave them freedom from getting frazzled over every decision.

In her book *Balanced: Finding Center as a Work-at-Home Mom*, Tricia shares the list they came up with:

To provide a godly homeschooling education for our kids.
To sign up each child for only one extracurricular activity a
year so we could have more time together
To have dinner as a family to build our family bond
To train our children how to be part of the family unit and
do chores
To connect and serve in our local church
To have reading time together as a family at night
To see what God was doing in our lives and follow Him.[30]

Establishing principles for their priorities served as a scheduling filter as a family. "Should we sign our son up for soccer? No, because he already played basketball this year. Should we limit television-watching in the evening? Yes, because our priorities are face-to-face dinner, chores, and reading time. Should we help start a children's ministry at our church? Yes, because it's how their family can serve together."

Their new system had other benefits. Tricia didn't feel as guilty now: she could distinguish between what was important versus what was "good" for their family. She felt freer from the pressure to accept writing assignments or other commitments only to prove herself. The family experienced more peace and centeredness. When she started to feel overburdened again, she knew where to start with re-instilling peace again.

Dare to Define What's Important to You

Everything can't be equally important all the time in every season. Step back and make a list of things and people that get first dibs on your time and your emotional, financial, and mental resources. Where do you feel pulled in two directions? What core value might be at the heart of these nonessential claims on your time and resources?

PART IV

THE PREPARATION

18

NAME YOUR PATHS:
Objectifying Options Uncovers Relevant Info

"When you commit to "just do something," you move in the right direction. Once you're moving in a direction that is aligned with the character and heart of God, you find God's personal mission for your life begins to come into focus."

—Erwin McManus, *Chasing Daylight*

Indecision is a jungle of information, fear, and uncertainty. Its twisted vines have an uncanny power to muddle what we want, limiting what we think are our only options. So, if we find ourselves trapped in this jungle, unable to find a path and move forward, one approach is to objectify it. First, we can label what kind of crossroads this is. Giving it a name and isolating your choices helps simplify the decision process.

For starters, you could ask what this crossroads is about:

A problem to solve?

An opportunity to experience?

A direction to choose?

A change to navigate?

A steppingstone to whatever is next?

A common crossroads conundrum my clients encounter is trying to figure out what to do with their life. They've felt the spark inside when they use their gifts and strengths, but when seasons change, they feel caught—even depressed—between the obligation of responsibility and the desire to feel alive.

PERMISSION TO IDENTIFY YOUR OPTIONS

"I'm not sure how to work on this, but I'm in a transition," Carla said. She had asked me to help her figure out a career after being a stay-at-home mom for years. "My husband would prefer it if I bring in some income for our family. My kids don't need me around as much now that they've finished high school. And we could use the extra money to put them through college. But . . ." Carla paused as though she would get in trouble for saying her next words aloud. "I'm not ready to let go of this season. I love being there for my kids, and the thought of getting a regular job drains me."

"What do you really want here?" I asked. I'd learned the value of letting people clarify what they want themselves rather than shortchanging them with my assumptions.

"I know I'm called to teach God's truth to women. I love the idea of teaching in some way, but that seems like a distant dream for me. I want the freedom to do what I want to do and not be focused on earning money at some mundane job. But it doesn't seem fair to chase my dreams at the expense of our family."

"What brings you joy right now?" I asked.

"Well, I've been volunteering in a couple areas of a home care agency I love, and that has been good for me. There's one aspect I'm not enjoying much, but I kind of feel obligated to continue because they're depending on me. I've learned a lot. I love working with the families, but the scheduling part drains me."

I dug further, and we wrapped up the call with some practical steps she could take to explore other passions. Before we hung up, Carla admitted she thought we would decide on a goal that day and work on the option she dreaded the most—finding her a job.

I laughed. "There's no point in that. This isn't about simply picking something and running with it. If it were that easy, you would have done it already. Before you can dive into a plan, you've got to figure out what you want on the other side of this transition and what some clear options could be."

"That sounds about right," Carla said, relieved. "I'm just not ready to up and make huge transitions yet."

When we know life can't continue as it is and yet we don't know what we want, we feel pressure from both ourselves and others to figure it out as quickly as possible. Carla's crossroads had a few paths she could explore:

- jobs she could enjoy that would still supplement the family's income

- ways to make money for her kids' college fund

- dormant gifts and passions that would bring a fresh sense of purpose in a new season

But for her, the paths were overgrown by conflicting desires, a sense of loss from leaving behind a season she loved, and fear of letting others down. Like most of us, she was most clear on what she *didn't* want. The weeds of fear limited her view of the paths available to her. Once she felt she had permission and a safe space, she could discover her options and choose a path to pursue.

CLEARING THE WEEDS

Tracey felt weary after a couple years of tough transitions, shifting from career to motherhood and dealing with renovations after a flood. Tracey's husband saw the toll it was taking on her and wanted her to feel like she was thriving again, so he encouraged her to find support.

When we met, she admitted she was starting to feel signs of depression. That scared her: she knew that succumbing to depression would take a toll on her husband and her little ones. Being a mom to toddlers didn't feel natural to her, and she felt scared that that meant she wasn't a good mom. Because of her husband's long, stressful hours at work, simple house repairs were up to her, and she felt guilty that she was not motivated to deal with them. On top of that, she was grieving the loss of a career that had given her an outlet to excel in her strengths. Without much control over external circumstances, she thought uncovering a dream for the next season of her life would help her get through this one. She assumed it to be a career but was open to anything that felt hopeful.

"Let's brain dump," I said in our first coaching session. "What are the dreams—big and little ones—you've filed away that you want to do someday?"

She started listing the things that brought her joy in the past and things she had imagined herself doing one day. As she talked, I began noticing similarities in some of the things she listed, plucking them out from the weeds of "I should" and "if . . . then." I jotted them down on a notepad, drawing a Venn diagram of overlapping circles around her words related to family, creativity, helping others, and her talents.

I laid down my pen, showed her the notepad, and leaned back. "What do you see here?"

She fell quiet as she looked over my scribblings.

I sensed emotion stirring in her as silence lingered.

"These are all expressions of who I am," she said, getting choked up. "This isn't so much about a career as living a fulfilling life." She went on to point out which dreams were the safe, nice-to-have ones and which ones were the scary, God-called dreams. The God dreams were the ones that others had affirmed in her the most but were also where she felt the most inadequate.

Over the next couple of weeks, she spent time exploring ideas for each of the clusters on the dream page. It didn't take long to notice she found more ideas around the areas she had identified as God-called dreams. We listed practical ways she could stay connected with people in her field and nurture her leadership skills, and she looked more encouraged each time we met.

Dare to Expand Your Options

First, define what your crossroads is about. Is it a problem, an opportunity, a direction to choose? Is it a steppingstone to the next goal?

Next, list the ideas you could explore further. Depending on your crossroads decision, these could be things you used to love, want to try, or excel at or things that energize you. After you write your list, challenge your creativity: what are three more options you could consider? Finally, be honest with yourself. What options scare you the most, and why?

19

FIND YOUR STYLE:
Overpowering Overwhelm Begins with Identifying Relevant Intel

When paralyzed at a crossroads, our stress is often centered around the pieces we don't know. We worry about the future. We seek to make the unknowns known. We try to pin down the things we can't control. How can we look at our paths from a place of hope rather than fear? How do we find out what we don't know? And once we find ourselves along the bunny trail of research and unlimited opinions, how do we recognize the information pertinent to our unique path?

I've noticed five inefficient approaches to gathering the information we need. Maybe you find yourself getting stuck in one or more of these styles.

Incapacitated Gatherers
Research is your happy place. New passion? Bring it on, baby.

You watch the YouTube videos, Google the top ten blogs, devour books on the subject, survey your social media following, and sign up for the samples and freebies. And after devouring all the information, you feel a little dazed.

Once you get your bearings again, you venture on the web to look up one more tidbit. After all, maybe that's the one piece that might ignite the clarity you need to make the decision. One more option gets added to your list. One more nuance complicates the options you already have. None of the options are quite saying what you want them to say. What if that missing information is the piece that would make all the difference? How do you wade through all the advice, stories, and considerations when you still don't really know what's on the other side of this decision?

Your brain starts shutting down again, and you find yourself in the classic case of analysis paralysis.

Intermittent Gatherers

You begin your research with finding some interesting tidbits. A blog sparks your curiosity, so you click on another link in the article, which leads you to a video. The video is enlightening, and YouTube has a list of suggested videos for you to watch, so you binge watch the next four. One gets you thinking about another angle of your original ideas, so you open another tab and begin another search. In the process you see the Facebook link in your bookmarks bar and remember you had a question to ask a friend. You open Facebook. The little bell dangles, letting you know there are fifty-two updates you haven't seen yet. May as well catch up while you're there, so you quickly scan the feed for anything important you might have missed. Meanwhile, the sound from the video still playing in the other tab catches your attention, so you click back over.

By the time you realize dinner is burning and log off, you've learned a dozen intriguing nuggets of information, but only one of them is helpful in your decision journey. Later that night you start the process all over again.

Ignorant Gatherers

You get overwhelmed before you even start. Just the thought of wading through stories, articles, and books sends you to your secret stash of chocolate and Earl Grey tea. Where do you even start? How do you know what info to trust? What do you do with all that info once you have it? *There's something to be said for "ignorance is bliss,"* you think as you turn on Netflix for an evening binge.

Impromptu Gatherers

Hands-on interaction is your jam. You don't have the time or attention span to look through a bunch of facts. There's no overthinking with you. You'll act on the first idea that's worked for someone else and figure it out along the way. Unfortunately, the "clarity comes with action" motto has its downside. The process takes longer than you think, and halfway through the project you peter out, realizing it's not what you wanted. You try something else, then something else, until discouragement sets in and your resources run dry.

The dream still beckons, yet now that you've tried everything you can think of, you're feeling wrung out.

Inspired Gatherers

You're the inspiring person at the room, captivating listeners with brilliant ideas. The picture you paint of your dream can excite anyone. You talk about what you want to do, connect with people who know people, and show off your Pinterest boards. You have a plan for how you would get started, and it sounds like you know a lot. However, after months of conversation your listeners realize you haven't made any progress, and you wonder why they edge out of the conversation.

You get a high from possibilities, theories, and imaginings of success, but you lack the drive to follow through when details and discipline matter.

IS THERE ANOTHER WAY?

If you're like me, you haave a sinking feeling as you look at each type, realizing you can identify with more than one. Heck, I've been all five at different times—and sometimes all within one crossroads recon mission.

In an age where any information, opinion, or advice is accessible, we'll have to sift through this info. Naturally, we'll be weighing the pros and cons. So, which info is worth considering? How do you process all the facts, feelings, and opinions you encounter along the way? How do you choose between something good and something better if the decision doesn't seem obvious to you? How do you determine if the information is trustworthy? What if each option compromises one of your values?

Thankfully, there's a better way you can gather information and sift through it.

Intentional Gatherers

You have a clear understanding of the outcome you want on the other side of your decision. You've written it down, so it keeps you focused on relevant information. You're open, asking questions of people who've been there. You find out what the gaps and the needs are. You review facts, give yourself permission to feel what you're feeling, and recognize what those feelings are signaling. You check in with your faith and what God is saying—or not saying. You seek counsel from trustworthy people and know whose opinions to dismiss. And then you dare to decide by taking action, knowing you'll learn more along the way.

Everything you need to know to make a wise decision is at your fingertips. Whether you don't have enough information or have an avalanche of considerations, let's dig into some ways to shake off your overwhelm.

Dare to Notice and Uncover Relevant Info

Which style of info gathering can you relate to most? How
has it worked or not worked for you?

20

FACE THE FACTS:
Looking at Your Options

*"Knowledge is wisdom that comes from acquiring truth.
Insight is wisdom that comes from living out the truth
we acquire. Discernment is wisdom that comes from the
Holy Spirit's reminders of that knowledge and insight."*

—Lysa TerKeurst, *The Best Yes*

Dana had already made two huge crossroads decisions by the time we met. She worked for a painting company and hated it. It took a near drowning to prompt her to give her notice and open her own painting company, one that would run by the standards she valued. That decision was quick, and it felt right. The jobs started falling into place.

The next major life decision was different. She felt a growing call to go back to school to become a children's pastor. She had been helping out with the children's program in her church because no one else had stepped up to do it. Many people appreciated how dedicated she was, but they didn't see her as a leader. She struggled with setting clear boundaries and keeping the kids and volunteers in line. Yet she was grateful for the impact mentors and pastors had had in her life while living in a lonely, unstable environment throughout her childhood. She felt a growing call to be that for others.

Beyond her fears and self-doubt, there were the practical things to think about. She was deep in debt, running her own business, and pouring ten hours a week into the children's program. How could she handle school payments and still pay off her debt? How could she find the time and energy to manage her painting contracts, invest in the kids at her church, and study? How would she maintain her health, which often buckled under stress? Did she have what it would take to get into school and keep up with the courses?

There are three forces that may propel you to consider a crossroads when you would otherwise stay on the safe, familiar path: a crisis, a call, or curiosity.

The first one propelled Dana into her first crossroads decision. The latter two moved her into her second. The call to impact children made her curious about what it would take to go back to school. Insecurity tried to minimize her potential. Doubt taunted that she was only a volunteer program coordinator, not a leader worth respecting. But despite the heckling, step by step she found the answers to the questions her curiosity and call were asking.

When overthinkers consider a major shift in life such as a move or a career change, the plethora of implications swarm our minds at once. Overwhelm settles in like dense fog. How do we uncover what's relevant so we can be confident we're evaluating information based on hope instead of fear?

Change happens one step, one choice at a time. Sometimes you simply need to write down what's in your head so you can look at the facts on their own. By assessing each option separately, it's easier to see which ones you'll be able to figure out on your own, which areas you'll need help in, and which ones you'll need to research. You'll also identify what seems impossible and would require a new approach to doing life.

Information

What do you need to know to make a wise decision? Where can you find this information? The information itself is unbiased. It is what it is. What is the practical truth in your reality? What are the expectations and assumptions *by* you and others? *Of* you and others?

- financially
- relationally
- emotionally
- geographically
- mentally
- physically (health, time, ability)
- intellectually (education, learning)
- spiritually
- environmentally (space, time)

Insight
- What do you need to consider in light of your past experience?
- Who else has done something like this, and how were they able to achieve it?

Impact
- Who will this decision impact?

- How will this impact them and you (consequences, opportunities, challenges, costs, gains)?

- What would be the short-term and long-term impact?

Dana found her answers by asking people who had already been down that path, listening to people who had challenged her to grow in the past, and seeking out a life coach who had an objective perspective. She contacted schools and talked to other students who had done the work. She calculated her budget, cut her expenses, and figured out what income she would need to pay for one course at a time as well as pay down debt. Realizing hiring help would give her more time for studying, she made a list of people she trusted and hired one of them within a week. Googling the best ways to pay down debt, she came up with practical ways and a timeline to pay down her debt and save money. She also talked to her doctor about how much stress her body could handle.

The key to collecting relevant information is to be honest with yourself. Emotions will come up, and we'll talk about that next. But first, you have to be honest about what you want and what could be possible beyond your doubts, beyond your own perspective.

WHAT ARE THE GREMLINS SAYING?

It's easy to believe the myth that the information phase is about collecting as much information as possible. The Perfectionist gremlin tells us, "You need to be thorough. Don't miss anything that will make you screw up."

However, gathering information for the sake of information won't inspire a wise decision. The best reason for collecting data is to identify and evaluate your options.

Your brain will be biased in the process. Already formulating a theory, it's looking for data that will validate what it has already decided. It will naturally advocate for options that feel comfortable and familiar, compelling you to default to the path you've always taken. Often, this can be an efficient way to solve a problem.

But how well is the familiar and comfortable way of life getting you to where you want to be?

The very fact that you're reading this book means your ultimate desire hasn't been fulfilled by that path. Your dream destination, even if you're not sure what it looks like yet, beckons you to a new path. The gremlins Fear and Frustration will also invite themselves to the party, liberally offering their opinions.

Fear tells you, *"You were fine staying safe where you were. This change is too big, too different."*

Frustration chimes in, *"Is it really worth it? There's so much to learn; there are pros and cons to both sides. How are you supposed to figure this out?"*

Elizabeth Gilbert had been writing for years before her book *Eat Pray Love* became wildly popular. In her book *Big Magic* she reflected on how much Fear interfered with her creativity after dealing with the pressure of a successful book—something she had dreamed of for years. She said she had to move Fear out of the driver's seat and ban it from backseat driving.[31] At your crossroads you could say, "Fear and Frustration, thank you for your input. It has been noted, but at this stage I'm only collecting information. I'm not deciding either way until I've looked at all the facts. I've done things your way for a while. I'm going to give my desires a fair chance, check things out for myself. So, hush for now. When I'm ready for your opinion, I'll ask for it."

If you're a pro at tuning out their nattering, and research makes your heart sing, then go for it! Only remember, your mission here isn't to collect as much information as possible but to position yourself to choose a path. So much of what you'll need to know for your journey you won't discover or understand until you start.

MINING FOR FACTS

Here's an approach I've used when I feel muddled and stuck:

1. **Inventory the facts.**
   Write down your facts on separate sticky notes or index cards. This allows you to survey them in different arrangements later on. Simply take what's in your head and put it onto paper.
2. **Identify options**.
   To help you stay objective, think of your options as if they were for someone else. Get crazy enough to jolt yourself out of your funk.
3. **Sort the options and facts**.
   Depending on the nature of the decision, this could be a pros and cons list, an options chart, a mindmap, or a "yes or no" list. Here you're acknowledging how a piece of information is leaning in a particular direction.
4. **Rate each option and fact.**
   Using a scale from one to five, jot down how much each matters to you (or scares you or overwhelms you). Sometimes Fear and Frustration are like attention-deprived toddlers who need a snuggle before they'll run off and play.
5. **Note questions and gaps.**
   As you survey your options, write down any information that seems to be missing. Is this a question you need answered to decide? Or is it something merely worth noting that you'll need to consider later on?
6. **Strategize new information collecting.**
   Throughout this process new info might present itself. Add it where necessary but be conscious of where you

might get sidetracked. If you feel it is relevant enough, set aside a different block of time to do it when your mind is fresh. Don't let new options steal your focus.

With your information recorded and sorted into options, you might already know what you want to do. Or you might be able to eliminate some options from further consideration. That's great! But remember, we still have more information to collect beyond the mere facts. Let's move on to that before we evaluate your options.

Dare to Face Your Facts

What do you already know about the change you're considering? What do you need to find out more about? What do you need to let go of?

21

YOUR FEELINGS ARE TALKING:
Listening to Your Heart, Head, Gut, and Body

"We change our behavior when the pain of staying the same becomes greater than the pain of changing."

—Dr. Henry Cloud

IF FEELINGS ARE FICKLE, WHAT CAN I TRUST?

Perfectionism had me convinced that making wise choices was about black and white, right and wrong, and common sense. I was hungry to be good and to do good. People around me were making dumb choices and complicating issues that seemed so obvious to me. When I turned nineteen, I emerged from naive simplicity into, well . . . adulthood. Suddenly, decisions weren't so straightforward. I could relate to the mire of quandaries others had described.

My insecurity also spiked when Bible verses like Jeremiah 17:9 (NIV) played in the back of my mind: "The heart is deceitful above all things and beyond cure. Who can understand it?"

Did that mean I couldn't rely on my own judgment? I desperately wanted God to tell me every single step, especially when I was trying to figure out where to go to school. I felt self-doubt after my marriage fell apart, and when I knew I would eventually start dating again.

Sometimes I thought I heard what He was saying, and things turned out disappointingly. Other times He seemed silent. Not knowing what to count on in these times was enough for me to shove the dilemma away and read a novel or watch TV to numb my feelings.

I thought my ability to hear from God was the problem. I had no idea how much my interpretation of my feelings was affecting my life. If I woke up feeling cloudy, I would give in to the feeling and continue to feel sluggish the whole day.

What I didn't realize yet was that feelings tell us how we're interpreting the facts. They reveal the meaning we've attached to them. Often that meaning feels like facts because we're so used to the way we think. It is like when you would visit a friend's home as a child, and they had different rules and different family habits than yours. Sometimes they seemed delightfully appealing, and other times they got uncomfortably foreign. You didn't even know there was a different way to do family until you encountered it.

Here's another example. Let's say you texted your friend Tina earlier today. That's the fact. She hasn't responded yet, and you feel your anxiety rising with every thought. *Is she mad at me? Am I not important to her? Doesn't she respect that I need an answer?* Later, you find out she had dropped her phone in the toilet and never saw the message. The meaning you attached to not receiving a text was set around your expectations (she should have answered your text right away), the story you're telling (if I don't get the response in my expected timeframe, she must be thinking *xyz*), and your beliefs (my value is attached to how long it takes someone to respond to me).

Say another friend texted Tina that day at the same time. When she didn't hear back right away, her response was, *Hmm, Tina hasn't responded yet. She must be having a hectic day. I'll check in with her tonight.* Different expectations prime you for different reactions.

If my feelings could be affected by everyday situations that weren't really a big deal, how would I handle my emotions at lifechanging crossroads? I didn't know what to do when I felt vulnerable and didn't trust my gut, so I shut out my emotions and relied on rationale.

WHAT IS YOUR HEAD TELLING YOU?

No surprise, your head is the rational brain comparing pros and cons. It likes using language such as "I should" and "I think." It assembles metaphors, recognizes patterns, and composes narratives with your information. When it's functioning at its best—not too stressed, not too relaxed—your mind is resourceful, easily coming up with new strategies.

This is the brain I wanted to count on in my decision-making. Not a fan of uncertainty, I thought laying out the facts would lead to certainty and a decent decision. I didn't know then about a neuroscientist named Antonio Damasio. He studied people with an injury to the part of the brain where emotions are generated. These people seemed normal in every way except that they didn't have the ability to feel emotions. You might figure decisions would be quicker and simpler without complicating emotions. Nope. He was surprised to discover that their decision-making ability was seriously damaged. Even though they could logically describe options and what they should be doing, in reality they couldn't make decisions such as what to wear or eat. Reason and emotion are meant to complement each other in decision-making.

Thankfully, we're designed with three centers of intelligence: the heart (feeling), head (thinking), and gut (instinct or intuition). Each has its own neural pathways in the body, sending messages to each other, and they are all at work in how you relate to what's happening around me, even if you don't understand how.

WHAT IS YOUR HEART TELLING YOU?

"It's a matter of the heart." It's not only a wishy-washy figure of speech reserved for romantic comedies. In the heart intelligence center, we process what's important to us, how we feel about our goals, dreams, and desires, how we relate to others, and what we do to feel connected.

If you're someone like me who has been guided by the *should's* and systems of the brain, or if you tend to make decisions based on what you instinctively know in your gut, maybe you need a reminder that your heart needs to have a say in your direction too. Tuning in to what you want, knowing your values, and being others-centered keeps your sense of purpose alive. It's why in the earlier chapters we started with exploring your dreams and desires. Snuff out your feelings or downplay them, and you'll pay a price later.

When I felt confused by my emotions, I either succumbed to them or shoved them away. I made them the problem, somewhat like placing duct tape over the warning lights in the dashboard of my car. It was lifechanging when I discovered negative feelings could be signals alerting me that something important to me needed attention.[32]

Understanding this liberated me from a heavy blanket of melancholy to make decisions from a place of wholeness.

In my early thirties, emotions enveloped me like a thick fog. Barely able to distinguish one from another, it didn't occur to me to talk to anyone about them. I didn't even know where to start. For a while I willed my way through them, eventually secluding myself in my apartment for days in listless, low-grade depression.

One day, unable to put words together in my journal about how I was feeling, I started mind-mapping my heart and thoughts. Words, circles, and lines filled the page until clarity crystallized.

I was feeling the absence of a partner. I had no one with whom to navigate my purpose and share my dreams and daily moments. I felt the imbalance from working a lot but not taking time to enjoy activities I thought were fun (which often wasn't what my peers thought was fun). And I noticed the dynamics of being in leadership and not being free to process my thoughts with just anyone. At the root of it all, I was feeling disconnected and lonely, wishing for someone who truly understood me.

Well, that last one should be easy, I thought. *Who do I know I could hang out with?*

As I thought through the names of people I knew, no one's company quite seemed adequate to draw me out of my funk. The only One I knew who could meet me on that level was God.

So, I flooded the apartment with my favourite uplifting worship music. I turned off the lights and soaked in the music for a while. Then I read my Bible and started writing in my journal. Normally my journal entries are my prayers to God. This time I asked Him to speak to me. I longed for a soul-level conversation, not a head-level conversation.

After an hour or two I felt completely different. Peace and contentment filled my heart. I felt known, loved, and understood. What a glorious contrast to my confusion and numbness!

I wrote my awakening in my journal:

When I'm feeling melancholic, listless, and lonely, it's my signal that I'm first longing for God to fill my heart. People or a project won't cut it.

Some cobwebs of loneliness clung to me though, and I couldn't quite shake them off. I realized I had isolated myself for too long. Now that I felt filled, I needed to find people to hang out with. This time, the step was an act of wisdom rather than one of desperation.

The insights of that day empowered me. I had never realized how often I allowed myself to isolate myself in a cloud of melancholy for days at a time until I knew how to recognize my pensive sadness and do something about it immediately.

What are your signals?

First, it helps to name what you're feeling, even getting specific about the nuance in each feeling cluster.

Happy Joy Bliss Delight Elated Excited Energetic Enthusiastic Creative

Content Peaceful Awe Marvel Grateful Thankful Serene

Afraid Numb Scared Fearful Paranoid Skittish Uncertain Petrified Terrified Quaking Hesitant Unsure Guilty Wary Anxious

Curious Wonderment Awe Inquisitive

Incompetent Inadequate Incomplete Doubtful

Anger Frustrated Confused Mad Seething Bitter Resentful Peeved Annoyed Prickly Disgusted Irritated

Sad Depressed Disappointed Defeated Dismal

Hurt Ashamed Betrayed Insecure

Next, as you consider your Dare to Decide information so far, what could your emotions be signaling?

Anxiety — "Beware" or "move away."[33]

Sadness — "It's time to grieve and let go."

Uncomfortable — "I might not be safe. Get ready to move or change something."

Fear — "Get prepared to deal with something that's about to come."

Hurt — "An expectation I have has not been met," or "I feel pain and a sense loss."

Anger — "A rule that's important to me has been violated (by me or someone else)," or "I've got to deal with an issue."

Frustration — "I'm doing the same thing over again and expecting a different result."

Disappointment — "Heads up! An expectation or an outcome I have won't happen now."

Guilt — "I compromised one of God's or my own standards."

Inadequacy — "I need to do something to become more confident or competent, or I need to realize I'm enough."

Overload — "It's time to reevaluate what is most important to me, distinguish between necessity and desire, and prioritize my list."

Maybe you'd find it helpful to recognize your positive feelings and their messages too. Because I could be so bound by responsibility and perseverance, I didn't realize how much I had numbed some of my positive feelings. When I found myself close to burnout, I gave myself permission to pursue more fulfilling projects by paying attention to the last times I had felt happy, satisfied, or energized.

Happiness — "All feels well with the world. I'm enjoying this. I'm in the right spot at the right time."

Satisfaction — "This was *so* worth the effort."

Energized — "I feel inspired to focus and act on something."

So, you might be wondering, are these messages always trustworthy?

I had to learn to examine my instinctive interpretation of the emotions—positive and negative. When we see or hear something, it triggers an emotion, and we respond according to how we interpret this. It can happen so fast that we don't even realize how we got from one point to another.

One month, I kept waking up feeling irritated and upset. First, I tried shaking it off by giving myself a pep talk and moving on with my day. After a few mornings of frustration, I paused to wonder why I kept feeling so bothered for no apparent reason. I realized each time I woke up in a funk, I had been having similar dreams. Backtracking further, I reflected on what I had been doing and thinking the night before. Sure enough, each time the trigger was the same. I even thought I was doing something noble and spiritual. After all, I was praying for someone. But as I worked through the emotions and their signals, I saw I needed to change how and when I prayed for that person. Once I made those changes, the dreams stopped, and I woke up in a much better mood.

Your emotions can be valuable sources of information at your crossroads, starting with self-awareness. What emotions have you been feeling lately? What messages are those emotions signaling to you?

WHAT IS YOUR GUT TELLING YOU?

As an avid NCIS viewer for years, whenever I hear the phrase "go with your gut," I think of Leroy Jethro Gibbs. He is the strong, silent, word-minimalist type. His marine training sharpened his ability to make quick decisions that didn't always seem logical in the moment, but his team knew his gut was never wrong. I admired the way others trusted his instincts.

Otherwise known as your primal brain or *intuition*, the gut brain cares mainly about your identity (who you are at your deepest core) and staying safe. It guards boundaries, satisfies hunger, and avoids pain and discomfort. It's also what drives you to act on the information you receive, like those emotions we talked about. That's because it's tuning into the subliminal external messages in your environment and memories of what you've seen, experienced, heard, and felt in the past.

When you're centered somewhere between stress and boredom, your courage comes alive. You trust your instincts, even if they don't seem logical, and you have peace with whatever the journey brings. But if you've experienced trauma, or if your gut has been frazzled with too much hustle, you'll feel more on edge. Your gut's primal survival mode—and your cortisol and adrenaline—take over, prompting you to fight, freeze, flee, or appease.

When you're in that stress mode, to tune into your gut's honest voice you'll need to calm your nervous system. The simplest way is through deep belly breathing.

Breathe in . . . one . . . two . . . three . . . four.

Breathe out . . . one . . . two . . .three . . . four.

Silence the thoughts so you can simply *be*. Nature walks, yoga, and music also help me with this. Others use meditation, kayaking, or journaling to find their way past the noisy thoughts and emotions to inner stillness.

And when you get to that quiet place, a deep, subtle *knowing* often settles in. Maybe it's not the full clarity you're looking for, but you know your next step or what direction to take. You might not know how you're going to get there, but you connect with a resolve inside that you weren't sure you could trust before.

That intuition found its voice when I was at a crossroads of what to do about my day job. I had enjoyed my place there for years, developed trust, rapport, and experience, but my heart called me to take leadership and purpose coaching more seriously. That meant investing money, losing my low profile, and becoming more visible. By that time I was remarried with a baby, and fear had me jumping to worst-case scenarios— mainly that we would invest money, not get a timely return on that investment, lose our home, and have to move into my in-laws' dingy basement.

So, I went there.

Well, not literally.

I gave fear permission to accept the worst-case scenario, but I weighed it against the risk of never trying. That's when my intuition shifted. Suddenly, I realized I'd be okay with a worst-case scenario fate if it meant I'd given it my all and gained the richness of experience in the journey. It was an exciting, startling moment for me. I realized I finally felt that staying safe and comfortable was far more uncomfortable than trying and potentially failing.

When you still your mind and spirit, what quiet inner knowing rises up?

WHAT IS YOUR BODY TELLING YOU?

Let's say you're the type of person who's determined to finish your race to the bitter end—because you're not a quitter. Or maybe you're sinking fast in the quagmire of indecision and can't get out. If you are used to relying only on one intelligence centre—the mind, the heart, or the gut—at some point something will feel off. Ignore these long enough and there's another centre of intelligence that will pull rank.

Body sensations. Your body reacts to things it sees and senses before your mind realizes it. You might lean in toward someone you like when you meet them or step back if there's someone who acts nice, but you simply don't trust them.

Our body also processes our emotions, even when we think we're okay. Let's say you recently graduated with your master's degree, and it's time to apply for jobs in your field. You've had time to think about the different types of jobs you would like, the ideal schedule you would enjoy, the tasks you would prefer. Spiritually you feel at peace; you've chosen not to be stressed. Your bank account is reminding you that you need a paycheck soon, and after applying for a bunch of jobs, you find yourself doing a lot of waiting.

While one part of your brain has chosen peace and trusts that things will work out in the right time, another part of your brain knows something could go wrong. When your body starts tensing, your brain smugly says, "I told you so," and ramps up the alarm. Now your body physically has to process those emotions somehow. Since how we want to feel and what we want to avoid feeling impacts our little choices and big decisions, this is worth knowing.

When I made a decision to step into coaching as an official thing—make it a business, not just a side hobby—I knew I would need help, so I invested in an online business coaching program—the most money I'd spent aside from buying a car or making a down payment for a house. It was four intense months of market research, writing content, making a website, creating a mini course, and gathering the gumption to put it out into the world.

Because I had already decided to commit to the process, I felt more resolve than fear. By the fifth month I launched a mini course . . . and crashed. I had no energy to push through the launch and felt all the familiar symptoms of burnout I experienced in my early twenties. Crying over everything. No energy to do anything. Low hope. No big picture. Depression. My shoulders and neck were rock-hard from hunching over a computer sometimes twelve hours a day. My hip felt out of place, so stretching and walking was uncomfortable. Finally, my jaw slipped after a disagreement with steak, leaving me only eating smoothies and soup for a few days.

I booked an appointment with my osteopath.

As soon as Kaitlin started working on me, she said, "Your body isn't very happy with you. Have you been stressed?"

Talk about an understatement.

She pressed her hand lightly over my abdomen. "You know fear is associated with the kidney, right?"

I already knew that when my hip goes out, so does my kidney. Or vice versa. But I didn't know about a fear connection. However, I did know scientists and health professionals are identifying patterns linking certain emotions to diseases in the body. If any emotions like anxiety, anger or unforgiveness are held in the body long-term without being felt, permitted, and released, then these emotions can wreak havoc on certain organs and show up as predictable diseases.[34]

My throat thickened as I swallowed. Did this mean I was in denial about feeling courageous?

"Well, that's disappointing," I told her. "This fall I've been working mega hours to pursue a dream. I thought I'd made progress being brave."

We chatted about pursuing dreams, and she told me cool stuff about how the brain and body work together. I'm not a very woo-woo person, but she explained it well, and I had heard enough stories to know there's more to how our bodies work than we can see.

She explained that manual osteopathy works not only with the lymphatic system but also with the brain. The technique releases soft tissues and fluids, which help the body heal emotional memories. It helps the brain learn new ways of thinking and helps you become the better person you want to be. By the end of our hour of chatting, I felt understood for why I had worked so hard instead of judged for not taking care of my body sooner.

Kaitlin finished with pressure points at the back of my head and recommended I add some relaxation practices back in my life. Then she said, "Your kidney was the least of your concerns. Each body has its default place where stress goes. A month ago, maybe your body sent the stress to your hip and kidney because that's what it normally does. But as you began to remap your brain, your body had to find another area to put its stress—your adrenal glands and neck."

Tears of hope welled in my eyes. I was overreacting from being at the end of my rope, but the kidney-fear correlation had bothered me the whole hour. It meant a lot that she acknowledged my body processing my stress differently. I had worked hard to shift my fear into courage. Somehow, it renewed my hope to continue believing in my dreams instead of living in my fear and weaknesses.

What is your body saying to you?

If your crossroads means a major shift in your life, don't underestimate the impact that will have on your body, emotions, and mind. The information your feelings send you could be grief for a part of yourself that you're leaving behind to make room for what's better. You might be feeling doubt because you've never done something like this before. Feel what you're feeling. Give yourself space to sort it out and take care of yourself so you can keep moving forward, becoming the person your dream needs you to be.

Dare to Listen to Your Feelings

When feelings surface, what do you tend to do? Stuff them back down? Magnify them with drama or anxiety? Try to reason your way out of them?

What is your head, heart, gut, and body saying to you right now?

22

FAITH CHECK:
When God's Not Talking

"The one who obeys God's instruction for today will develop a keen awareness of His direction for tomorrow."

—Lysa TerKeurst, *The Best Yes*

What seemed simple at one time has now become complicated.

To take one path forward, you leave another behind. Maybe one dream conflicts with another, and you realize you can't hold on to both any longer. As logical as it might be, you will grieve the loss of what could have been.

Maybe you've been on maternity leave, enjoying bonding with your baby, and you're torn apart inside because it's time to go back to work. Or you have a dream of more for your life, but your kids need you, and your aging parents need extra care. Maybe finances are tight, and that threat of scarcity constricts your ability to dream. Perhaps you already decided on your crossroads—you chose to go back to school or launch that business. You're on your own. You have no one else to help carry you financially, so you've had to work. You're burning the candle at both ends, and the wick is running out. You know you can't keep going like this. Something's got to give, and you're not sure what or how.

The challenges are real.

But there's another reason you're conflicted. You're not only a physical being; you're a spiritual being. You weren't meant to figure out life on your own strength or insight. It's not merely a decision you have to make. Sure, you care about the impact it makes on your family and those you've already invested in. You want whatever will have the best outcome for you and your family. You want to feel alive, not only believing you were meant for more but living it. Much like I realized my disconnected, lonely feelings meant I was craving quality time with God and friends, that's what your soul craves too.

The mind, heart, and gut thrive most when they are in a healthy state between being relaxed and being stressed. Tangible things help that balance—nutrition, exercise, rest, purpose. So does spiritual nourishment.

As a teenager and young adult, there was nothing I loved more than worship services at church. As music enveloped me, the inner defenses I had built up during the week broke down. Worries would shift into prayers. Gradually, the slow songs led me into a slow dance between God and my intuition. My babbling mind said its piece and ran out of things to say. My heart was present but quiet once I had a chance to feel what I was feeling. The core of me—the part that fights for me to be seen and accepted—found peace and security. It's in those moments I'd find the most clarity. They were breaths of inspiration, often one-statement exchanges.

Once, after I begged for a new adventure, He admonished me that He didn't have anything more to say until I took the last step I knew He had nudged me to take. Whatever that step was, I sidestepped it because it was unexciting, humbling, and uncomfortable, and I would have much rather dug into the more adventurous part of the journey ahead.

It was these kinds of moments of divine warmth and clarity that carried me through desert seasons when I didn't get the direction from God I begged for.

I didn't have a clue back then that there was any scientific proof or biblical teaching behind the process I went through to hear God's whisper. I only knew I experienced that process fullest with the hour set aside, the comfort of being surrounded by community, the fullness of the music, and a rich sense that God was present. As I grew older, moved around, and carried weightier responsibilities, the opportunities for this time with God changed. Different churches had different styles, or they would pause offering their evening worship services for a year or two. Or I'd volunteer to help in the nursery, sacrificing my own sacred time so sleep-deprived moms could get their hour alone with God.

That meant I had to be open to other ways of experiencing the peace and nourishment of God's presence. It wasn't that I didn't spend time with God throughout the week. I read my Bible in the mornings and chatted with God throughout the day. But it meant I had to get creative when my soul thirsted for deep wells of living water. If I didn't, it was easy to feel depleted from living up to others' expectations, toxic with worries and lonely from disconnectedness.

Other ways I'd bring my soul into God's presence include:

A morning walk
Long car rides alone
Journaling
Hikes in nature
Parking by a lake view with my CD player blasting
Guided prayers or meditations
Yoga with a God-centered perspective

Yet, creating space and a mind-quieting, soul-quenching environment wasn't the only way I discovered where to tune into what God was saying.

WHEN GOD DOESN'T SEEM TO HAVE MUCH TO SAY

As a teenager, somehow the simplicity of my faith in Him and my personality translated into striving to always be good. I didn't like the feeling of disapproval from anyone I loved, including God. I didn't want to screw anything up, so I felt hesitant to do anything unless I was absolutely sure He wanted me to do it.

This distilled my communication with God down to transactional prayers such as, "Should I do this or that?" or "Bless me as I do this," or "What do you want me to do?"

Those prayers seem spiritual, and a lot of people pray them. But they were all about me. They were all business. The more I prayed prayers like that, the more the silence yawned in response. I was trying to squeeze answers out of God like water out of a sponge so I could feel confident in my choices.

One of God's answers began a transformation in my perspective and approach to asking for God's input. The theme of my prayers of desperation that season had been, "God, what should I do with my life?" After months of frustration and feeling totally lost, God's quiet words parted the clouds of my mind. It wasn't an audible voice but a clear, succinct impression.

My daughter, I know your heart and your interests. You can do anything you want, and I'll be with you. I created you to make these choices. I never meant to make them all for you. I love watching you lean into your interests and discover what you can do.

What a relief to finally hear an answer! And how annoying. I pictured a wide open field. No paths to choose from. No specific destination on the other side. Just one wide open field with the massive sky and horizon in the distance. It was like God was showing me the immensity of my choices: I could cut any path, and He would make something from it.

I didn't know what to do with that, so I shoved the thought away and distracted myself for a while.

My landlord slipped the mail under my basement apartment door days later. The return address was from one of the schools I had written to inquire about one of their programs.

I saw it as a continuation of my conversation with God, as if He was saying, *Is this what you really want? Okay, let's explore it and see where this goes.* It gave me a way to eliminate options and begin moving in a direction.

Other times I'd settle into a time of waiting, drawing peace from the realization that if God wasn't worried that I needed a season of healing, or if my action plan wasn't working out, then I didn't need to be concerned either.

Over the years I've watched how faith-filled people interact with God in their decisions. What seems to trip them up? What gets God talking in decision-making? What actually happens as they start down one path but end up at an unexpected destination? Here are some of my observations.

1. Clues to God's desires are found in the Bible and in His character.

Sometimes people get caught up and stalled out by needing to discern His will when the information they need is right there. In other words, they make a big deal about needing to understand God's intention for them because it seems the right thing to do.

Think of a best friend you know well enough that you know exactly what they would do in a situation. You might even know what kind of advice they would give you. God is kind, forgiving, and just. He's proud of anyone who advocates for the marginalized. He remembers the forgotten and cares for the hurting. He's okay with letting you learn the hard way if that will renew trust in Him when you find yourself figuring life out on your own. If you have no clue what to do, find ways you can do things God loves and see what lights you up.

2. God can't steer a parked car.

This is what I learned in that defining moment at age twenty. Even though I heard that message from God and received that letter, I never did end up attending the school's program. The point hadn't been for me to choose whatever the heck I wanted. I realized later the purpose had been for me to get my butt in gear and make a decision. When I followed an option down any path, I would learn something new, gain a new perspective. One path would lead to another, and I would discover options I never knew existed. Often, I didn't see the ultimate path while I was lounging in my comfort zone. I had to get out there and discover what I didn't know I didn't know.

3. God values relationship over correctness.

That's not to say doing the right thing doesn't matter. The Bible says plenty of times that God values producing fruit in your life, doing good work, and accomplishing a mission. But His ultimate desire is relationship with us and for us to become more like him. That's why He went to incredible lengths to lead us to see the need to rely on Him instead of doing life on our own.

He wants to be part of our story, and He wants that story to help others realize the same thing. As a recovering perfectionist, this *aha* moment revolutionized my prayer life. I changed the questions I was asking God. Instead of asking, "What do I do about this, God?" I asked relational questions. "Father, where are you at work in my crossroads? What are you wanting to do in me? Who do you want me to inspire through my working this out? What do you love about this idea I'm considering?"

4. When God's doing His part and I'm doing mine, good things happen.

The frustration of including God in my decisions is wondering what's my part and what's God's part. Unfortunately, I overthink things and complicate them. I want to figure out my decision by thinking ten steps ahead. I fill time to distract myself from the frustration of not knowing. These approaches merely bog me down with stress, doubt, and distractions.

My part usually comes down to trusting God and doing what I know to do. Often, the little things I know to do are what I don't feel like doing. They seem insignificant and unproductive. Or the one thing I know I should do I avoid because it requires more humility and discipline than I'm willing to dish out. Yet submission and owning the steps I know to do are what end up showing me how God does His part. It empowers me with a peace that helps sift through the options and worries that fill my mind.

5. God dreams demand faith and His power.

If you've invited Jesus to lead your life, you're probably well acquainted with something God said thousands of years ago to the people He loved. These people had their own ideas about forgiveness, mercy, and justice. However, they were in a story much grander than their lifetime. They had no clue what God was up to. He summed it up this way.

> "For my thoughts are not your thoughts, neither are your ways my ways," declares the Lord. "As the heavens are higher than the earth, so are my ways higher than your ways and my thoughts than your thoughts."
> — Isaiah 55:8-9 (NIV)

We want the writing in the sky telling us what to choose and where to go. But are you sure you really want that?

In the Bible, every time God told people to carry out a specific mission, usually they didn't understand its significance or their own potential at that time. It highlighted their own weaknesses. It meant being misunderstood or mocked, often for decades. Noah was commissioned to build a boat for one hundred and fifty years when it had never rained before, and there was no way to get it to water when it was done. Moses was a misfit and a murderer with a fear of public speaking who ran away to the desert for a few decades before God sent him to free a million people from a tyrant. Deborah was invited to lead tribes in a culture where women did not have value or respect. Gideon was hiding when he was called into a mission with impossible odds. In the New Testament, Joseph was told to marry a pregnant girl who wasn't carrying his child in times when his family and community would have thought the worst of them if he did. Following the Holy Spirit's leading, the preacher Paul went to cities where he knew he would be beaten, imprisoned, or shipwrecked.

Having your path written in the sky is not the same as having the faith to follow that path.

6. Choose sanctification over success.

In today's culture I often hear the slogans "Become the best person you were meant to be" and "You were made for greatness" in the context of outward success and achievement. When I was young, pastors and teachers used big spiritual words like "sanctification" to explain this same concept. Things are sanctified when they are set aside for how God intended. God not only designed us. He invites us to create, lead, and participate in bringing restoration into our world. The audacious dream calling you is grand for a reason. It's part of what God will use to shape you into who He wants you to be. Failure develops us

> Having your path written in the sky is not the same as having the faith to follow that path.

more than success, so He's okay to use our mistakes in helping us grow. When we're up against a wall, He's not taken aback by our questions. He's thrilled to use our weaknesses to show off His strength when we finally realize we can't figure this out on our own. Our desperation is what leads to dependence on Him, and the end of ourselves is where He can begin.

The more we condition our heart, mind, and intuition with His desires, His nature, and His power, the more we recognize His presence at our crossroads, even if we don't hear His voice the way we want to.

WHAT IS THIS REALLY ABOUT?

I wanted to buy a house.

After living in apartments for thirteen years, I wanted to exchange my tiny balcony for a small yard where I could dig in some dirt, plant a little garden, and step out onto a patio in sunny weather. When my family came to visit and friends were in hard times, I wanted to offer an extra room for someone to crash overnight without worrying about pull-out couches, parking spots, and concerns of overstepping landlord rules. I longed to have a bright, open space with a sunny office where I could dream bigger (and where my bookshelves and writing desk weren't crammed into my bedroom). I wanted a place that had space to host a small group comfortably. I wanted a home I could be proud of, a place I could call mine, but I was single, living off a nonprofit salary, and renting out a room in my two-bedroom apartment to cover my bills.

Diligently I set aside bits of my paycheck each month, praying for a way to make this dream possible.

My third roommate moved out, causing me to dip into my savings to pay rent. Within the month a friend called and randomly asked if I would rent a room from her. She had bought a new home and was on her own trying to cover her own bills. After finally having my own place for a few years, renting a room on someone else's turf was less than desirable to me. But I couldn't ignore the coincidence after I had just been chatting with God about how to get creative about buying a home. Though this dream was far out of my comfort zone, I was tired of excuses, and I was ready to tackle obstacles head-on and figure out a way.

A couple months later the contents of my apartment were divided between a storage unit and this friend's attic bedroom suite. I had carved out a cozy corner to live in for the next year while I stashed away a couple hundred extra dollars each month and walked through what it could look like to own a home. Homeowner budgets. Financial assessments with an advisor, who said she was impressed with how much I had saved on my meager salary. A realtor showed me through cringe-worthy, crooked shacks within my budget just so I could see what was out there. But nothing came close to resembling a wise investment or having dream potential.

It was hard not to get discouraged, especially in the dim lighting of my attic corner. I was committed to an open mind and creative ideas, committed to busting through obstacles that year, so I kept looking for hope.

The answer came when a couple I knew said they were interested in us investing together in a student home near the local university.

Excitement and terror grew as we looked at homes with numbers higher than I had ever dealt with. But I loved the idea of partnering with people who had a better idea of what they were doing. I was eager to learn and grow through this. We found a "this is it" home, put in an offer, drew up the paperwork . . . and waited.

Within weeks the house offer fell through, and plans changed. My year living with my friend was overdrawn, and I had no idea what to do next. I was out of connections, gumption, and provision. I needed to find somewhere else to live but couldn't afford a home on my own. I had depleted all my hope and energy to take risks and think outside the box.

A friend invited me to move into a new apartment with her and her daughter. I moved in gratefully, but I felt betrayed by and disconnected from God.

One day, after a month of spiritual silent treatment and brooding, I faced God, arms crossed.

"I thought you wanted me to buy a house. To step out of my comfort zone. To take a risk. You were in this. It's why I took the leap and stretched way beyond my comfort zone. For what? Want to tell me what the heck this was all about?"

I half expected silence. Straightforward, enlightening answers hadn't exactly been my norm lately. But I sensed a simple response in my heart.

This was never about you buying a house. It was about deepening your trust in Me no matter how things turn out. You're going to need that strength soon.

Awesome.

I was not a happy camper with that response. But He was right.

I had never doubted He was leading me, even though I may or may not have freaked out numerous times. And having gone through that, I did trust him. He was up to something big in my life, and knowing He was preparing me for that gave me the peace I needed to rest in my disappointment.

From my perspective, chasing that dream had been more about proving myself and becoming someone who didn't miss out on life by playing it safe. Even though I hadn't bought a house in the end, I did become more resilient in uncomfortable situations throughout that season of my life.

From God's perspective, that adventure was about nurturing my trust in Him and seeing if I would obey, even when things didn't feel comfortable or sensible.

Your crossroads are opportunities to connect with God in fresh ways and trust Him. Though He cares deeply about you, He cares more about who you're becoming and your relationship with Him than your dream of becoming a success. He leans toward sanctification over success.

Dare to Connect with God

What has held you back from connecting with God on a heart level? Assuming you'll know how He'll respond? Fear of what He'll say or what you won't hear? Busyness? Trying to prove yourself or do it your own way? Shame? Protecting your heart from further pain? Dare to be open, and step, even run, closer to Him.

23

FRIENDS AND FOES:
Identifying Others' Roles in Your Story

A person's thoughts are like water in a deep well,
but someone with insight can draw them out.

—Proverbs 20:5 (GNT)

I knew it was smart to have input from others whenever I faced a big decision because I'd lived with the Proverbs ingrained in me.

"Get all the advice you can, and you will succeed; without it you will fail."

—Proverbs 15:22 (GNT)

"Stupid people always think they are right. Wise people listen to advice."

—Proverbs 12:15 (GNT)

What stressed me out was figuring out which advice to listen to and how to ignore unsolicited advice. I tended to adhere to any opinion stronger than my own. I would take the advice of someone I respected simply because I didn't want to let them down. When something didn't feel right for me, I would quietly dig in my heels. I would make my own choice, dreading the moment someone might confront me about it. Over the years as I watched how others handled criticism graciously, I grew more confident in establishing and communicating my boundaries.

When we're considering a shift we're about to make in our life, we're apt to hear a range of criticism, skepticism, and advice. For some reason, when we're about to change the norm in our life, people feel the need to comment. It will come from all sides—family, friends, and even strangers. Those whose support you the most might be the most critical. And the deepest wisdom might come from the most unexpected people.

Whether we've asked for it or not, we'll have to figure out what we do with the information people give us. It's going to trigger fear and colour our perspective on the intel we've already been weighing. If you're prone to people-pleasing, avoiding conflict, or perfecting everything first, navigating this part will be all the harder. So, how can you recognize the difference between wisdom, fear-based caution, and useless babble?

First, you can consider the source of the input. Second, as you instill your boundaries, you can develop tools to handle the unhelpful or unsolicited advice.

FINDING YOUR DARE TO DECIDE FRIENDS

These are people who have your best interest in mind. They care deeply for your character growth, your authentic potential coming alive, and building your legacy. This means they're okay with you being uncomfortable. They know growth comes from doing things differently than you have in the past. It might mean they believe in you more than they believe in your idea. It means they give you the space to contemplate a different future. They seek to understand your heart and destination instead of trying to find it for you.

Light givers

Honest yet gracious, light givers say what you need to hear, not necessarily what you want to hear or what *they* think you want to hear. They recognize you have greater potential than you're living right now, and they don't want you to stay in denial or ignorance. With your permission, they hold up a figurative mirror to show you who you truly are when you're blinded by doubt, near-sightedness or ego.

Mentors

Having travelled a path resembling the one you're facing, mentors share their experience because you've invited them to. They've faced similar risks and are living the outcome of their decision. They inform you of what you haven't experienced yet, filling in gaps in perspectives and providing useful information for you to consider. They help normalize the questions and feelings you have along the way.

Listeners

These friends give adequate space for you to process what you're thinking. By asking a question or two, listeners draw out clarity. They empower you to solve your own dilemmas. They realize their opinion is based on their limited perspective, so they keep an open mind. Understanding this decision is yours to own, they see the value of letting you wrestle it to the ground. They resist interjecting their unsolicited advice because they realize it would actually demean your competence in figuring this out.

Guides
Looking at where you want to go, guides lead you step-by-step along a segment of the path, which saves you the time and energy of figuring it on your own. While mentors tell you where and how to go forward, guides come alongside you.

Kindred spirits
You love these friends because empathetically understand you. The moment you're in their presence, something deep in your core relaxes because you feel known and understood. They're walking their own Dare to Decide path and crushing it amid their own fears and faith. When they listen to your story and you hear theirs, you both feel inspired and encouraged. Their enthusiasm refuels your energy when doubt steals your zeal.

Investors
Investors believe in you or your dream destinations enough that they become invested in the journey. Seeing the value of where you're headed, they might pay for a course, cover start-up costs, or offer free babysitting to release you to move forward. Because of this they make it possible for you to dream further than you might have otherwise.

Collaborators
Partnering with you in specific areas, collaborators share the risks, challenges, and opportunities. Together, your strengths and perspectives often balance each other out, strengthening your impact.

These Dare to Decide friends might show up in one or more of these roles. You might find them through books or podcasts, in person or online. They might walk alongside your whole journey or segments of it. Some will turn up at just the right time. In some seasons you might rely on God to fill all these roles in your life, but other times you might use God as your excuse. When you feel like you're doing your dream alone, it takes creativity and gumption to hunt down and invite someone into your story.

But what about when you're surrounded by people who seem intent to bring you down?

RECOGNIZING YOUR DARE TO DECIDE FOES

If those closest to you (whether in relationship or proximity) are haters, posers, or doubters, they might be why you have stayed stuck for so long. It's not that these people intend to crush your heart. They might simply be too caught up in their own narrative to recognize how they can support you in yours.

Do any of these types of people sound familiar?

Haters
Whether passive-aggressive or downright mean, haters often spew their black-and-white or religious remarks through email, social media, or rumours. They seek to be heard without understanding you and rarely want to engage in an open conversation to see a different perspective.

Posers
Posers toss out their opinions when they've never been down the path you're considering. They've never started a business or written a book but have loads of "expert" advice about how to start yours. They'll tell you what happened to their friend's dad's uncle and caution you against doing the same thing. Maybe they even claim they thought about doing something like what you're considering, then list all the reasons they didn't, as if these should be your reasons too. They know a little about everything and may sound enthusiastic about your idea, but they offer little of the experiential wisdom you need. Their words might sound insightful at the time, but after a

while the lack of substance holds you back from taking their input seriously.

Doubters

Darkening their life and commentary with negativity, doubters magnify your hesitations with their skepticism. Though they might tell you their concerns in the spirit of "realism," in reality they're anchored by fear. Often those who care about you feel threatened that they'll be left behind if you change for the better. When you feel alive, they become more aware of where they feel stagnant. Maybe they even feel disappointed with themselves for not pursuing their own dreams and don't want you to go through the same thing.

Call them out as Dare to Decide foes. Because if you make excuses for them, you'll stay stuck. It doesn't mean they're bad people or even have ill intent toward you. Here you are at this crossroads, ready to change the trajectory of your life. If you're not intentional about the people you surround yourself with and allow to influence you, you're doomed to walk in circles.

DEALING WITH WHAT OTHERS THINK

For many years I had a mindset of helplessness. When I was confident in what I had to do and why it mattered, I could be tenacious. But most of the time I felt like I could be undermined at any moment. Any strong opinion or intense personality could override me, and I hated it. Feeling like that only reinforced my victim mindset.

One day an *aha* moment empowered me in a way I needed desperately. I was on the edge of burnout. At work I habitually stayed late to finish projects. I could get more done in that hour after everyone left work than I could in an entire afternoon. I figured since I didn't have anyone to go home to, I may as well stay and enjoy the stillness. While the work culture celebrated going the second mile and adapting to last-minute inspirations, I was gradually establishing better boundaries. Perfectionism and over-responsibility were softening their grip on me. That week I promised myself I would leave on time so I could make a healthy meal and give my brain some breathing space.

I had been doing okay for a few days until a last-minute data entry project came up. Of course, the project was last-minute because a team member had not planned nor communicated well. Part of me wanted to let the consequences fall on the team member, who probably needed that wake-up call. However, I also realized that if this project were late, another team member wouldn't move on with his part, and it would impact hundreds of people. I wanted him to succeed, and that would mean me staying late. If I stayed late, I would feel annoyed that I had compromised my attempts to take care of myself. If I left early, I would feel guilty that I had left something undone and prevented someone from doing their best.

A familiar feeling of resentment bubbled up inside me. Yet again, I would head home alone, drained, with barely enough mental energy to throw together some nachos and crash in front of the TV.

You have a choice. No one is making you do anything. Pick your path and own it.

Those words cut sharply through my indecisive angst. Remembering how I had learned that emotions are signals, I realized resentment and guilt were alerts that my boundaries and values were being disrespected. Now that the feelings had done their job, I didn't need to hold on to them anymore. I could choose what I was going to do and do it cheerfully instead of feeling helpless.

I stayed and finished the project. Typically, I would just cover it up, not wanting to be a complainer, but this time I made a note to mention the irresponsibility to my supervisor.

Walking to my car, I felt proud I had given our team another win. Surprisingly, at home that night I had enough energy to throw together a healthier dinner. Letting go of resentment and resistance freed me up to enjoy the night.

Your crossroads decision is yours to own.

It will probably impact people who love you and those who are used to how you work with them, live with them, volunteer with them, and serve them. Others will undoubtedly have their opinions. You might be misunderstood or under-estimated, but ultimately your decisions are yours. Chances are you won't eradicate naysayers from your journey. In fact, you can count on it.

Every story needs resistance to strengthen the main charac-ter. Your Dare to Decide foes might be a source of the conflict, or they might reveal it. Each resistance is an opportunity for you to choose the kind of character you want to be, both in that situation and on the other side of your dream. What you decide might even be the proof they need to make changes in their own lives.

HANDLING UNSOLICITED ADVICE AND OPINIONS

So, how do you determine what input is actually helpful? First, let's look at why we ask for advice. Here are some things we might be looking for:

- **Approval or Connection**—asking for advice can be a way of drawing someone close to us when we feel disconnected.

- **Perspective**—we need other viewpoints to fill in gaps or broaden our outlook.

- **Validation**—we have learned not to trust our own judgment, so we believe someone else's input will validate ours or be better than ours.

- **Procrastination**—getting yet one more story or piece of info can be a subconscious ploy to avoid taking an action that might make us uncomfortable.

- **Certainty**—we're looking for a surefire solution before we go all in.

- **Support**—our decision will impact people in our sphere of influence, so inviting their input is an opportunity for them to process and participate.

- **Collaboration**—we need the skills and resources of others to accomplish our dreams.

The state you're in influences the kind of input you receive as well as how you respond to it. If you're feeling broken and weak, you're more likely to attract advice from people who want to fix you. If you connect your worth to what others think of you, your guard will be up when you hear criticism, and you might reject some of the wisdom that could help you move forward. However, beautiful things can happen amid your resolve to do what it takes to reach your dream destination, and when you stay open to grow through your strengths and limitations.

Even though unsolicited, untimely advice aggravates me, I still feel a magnetic pull to offer it. Why?

First, let's get real about why you and I like to offer advice.

- **Deflection**—we get uncomfortable when the circumstances of others shine a spotlight on our own unfilled dreams, comfort zone, and unwise choices.

- **Insecurity**—we see it as a problem and assume we're the ones who should fix it. Maybe it makes us feel more competent, or perhaps it's easier to live vicariously through them.

- **Unbridled enthusiasm**—we genuinely get excited for someone as we see their potential.

- **Judgment**—we view the world as black and white and feel the need to judge where it fits into the spectrum. Sometimes this is because it collides with our own failure to meet the standard.

- **Love**—we genuinely wish the best for someone and want to help.

Understanding what triggers you to give advice when it's not invited can help you be a little more objective when others dish it out. Reframing how you see someone's input won't necessarily keep you from feeling frustrated, but it will help you respond conscientiously instead of reacting. It helps to have some go-to strategies ready for different situations so that you don't have to default to defensiveness or shutting down. With practice you'll get better at discerning when to use ideas like these:

1. **Take advice as a compliment.**
   You're stepping out of the norm. Maybe you're pioneering a new path for others. One person's object of hate will be another's inspiration.

2. **Be silent.**
   Sometimes advice comes in the form of criticism, and it doesn't need a reply. Even on social media, maybe letting others speak up for you will have more weight than trying to defend your position.

3. **Consider the point.**
   Add it to your list of info to evaluate constructively.

4. **Surprise them with kindness.**
   Maybe you take the time in person or on the phone to hear them out and hear how they interpreted what you said.

5. **Prepare responses.**
   If you're caught in a conversation and need time to gather your thoughts for a genuine reply, come up with some lines you can default to. "Thanks for sharing that. I'll take it into consideration when I make my decision." Or, "It sounds like that worked well for you. Since we have different personalities/circumstances/values, I'm also looking at options that align with how I'm wired."

6. **Focus on your path, not the barriers.**
   If you keep focusing on the negativity, you'll find more negativity and stay blocked. Our energy goes where our focus flows.

7. **Outshine darkness with light.**
   Remember that most happy, successful people rarely put others down. They simply don't need to. They have better things to do with their energy. Seek out people and experiences that will flood your perspective with grace, hope, and possibilities, which will overflow onto others.

Dare to Name Your Dare to Decide Friends

Write a list of the people in your life who believe in you or support you in accomplishing your dream:

- Light givers

- Mentors

- Listeners

- Cheerleaders

- Guides

- Kindred spirits

- Collaborators

If you don't have any in a certain area, brainstorm who has been one in the past or who could have that potential. There's a time and season when each one is needed. Which ones do you need most right now? How could you intentionally set up more time with them or position yourself to meet one?

PART V

THE DECISION

24

MAKING SPACE FOR
THE BIG DARE:
God, Your Gut, or Gumption?

*"Time is working either for you or against you in terms
of your needed ending . . . Your brain needs to really get
it—that if you don't move, something bad is going to
happen, and also that if you do, you will get what you
desire. You have to break through the comfort level that
you are in, where you are settling for living in hell just
because you know all the names of all the streets."*

—Henry Cloud, *Necessary Endings*

I had spent a day with my coworkers exploring our per-
sonalities in the context of our team. In front of each one
of us was our Birkman[35] portfolio with a description and
a multicoloured graph. In our hands we held one sheet that
had our score for a dozen different ways we're wired, such as
Social Services (sensitivity to interpersonal dynamics) and
Artistic (sensitivity to the way things appear). One such rating
category was Persuasion. Each of us had to place ourselves in

the line-up according to our score. No surprise, the energetic, people-oriented, passionately-convince-anyone-of-anything guy proudly stood at one end of the line with his score of ninety-nine percent.

I meekly snuck into the other end of the line with my one percent.

We all had a good laugh, but that score bugged me for years. I thought that meant I was lame at convincing people to see things a certain way. Sure, I was the type of person who would get flustered in debates, but I was sure I had developed enough skill to inspire someone towards a better approach.

When I finally dug into understanding this attribute more, I realized it wasn't a matter of being able to persuade or not persuade others. It had to do with *how* people use words to motivate others. People with high scores of Persuasion get a kick out of being convinced into something—even expect it. Others don't have the patience or inclination to convince you of anything. And those of us with low Persuasion scores get highly suspicious the moment we feel we're being "sold to." It explains why I spent years avoiding the salesperson whenever I would enter a clothing store. I want the facts so I can evaluate the pertinent details. If I sense someone is trying to get me to buy a product or adopt an idea simply because they want me to, well, let's say that's when my husband pulls out the "stubborn" word.

When I learned this about my personality, I understood why I was so grateful for the insights in the book *Sway: The Irresistible Pull of Irrational Behavior* by Ori Brafman and Rom Brafman. It explained why I felt skeptical at my crossroads when an unseen force seemed to be at play. It also explained why listening to your gut might steer you to what seems familiar. A threat to your identity, reputation, or comfort zone will compel you to do what it takes to save it. According to the authors' research, undercurrents sway our decisions. Sometimes God gets the rap for it. Sometimes our gut does.

Sometimes we don't know how the heck we got swept off to where we ended up.

What you're up against is normal. The more aware you are of this, the more you can make your decisions with eyes wide open, not believing everything you see, feel, or hear. With that awareness you can make the best next choice you can at the moment.

How might you naturally be swayed as you face your crossroads?

Loss aversion. We tend to focus more on short-term consequences than longer-term effects, causing us to overreact when we consider potential loss. The more significant loss is to us, the more we fear losing what we already have. We don't want to let go, and we'll do our darnedest to avoid loss, even when it's financially, emotionally, or physically beneficial for us to do so.[36]

At your crossroads, loss aversion might sound like one of these statements:

They might disapprove if I _____, even though the thought of it makes my heart sing.

I want to believe this investment will pay off in a big way, but I can't afford it right now.

I don't know how much more I can take of this job, but what about my retirement plan?

Commitment also has a strong hold on us. When we're already committed to or invested in a relationship, position, or direction, it's hard to see better options. We would rather keep slugging through, even when facts might support letting go.[37] I'm a big sucker for this sunk cost fallacy.

What does commitment fallacy sound like at your crossroads?

I've already invested so much! I can't change my direction now.

I've come so far; I can't pull the plug now. Maybe things will get better.

Perceived value happens when we respond based on subjective context rather than objective facts.[38] If we see something with a label or a certain stigma, we treat it accordingly. This is what happened to violinist Joshua Bell, one of the finest musicians in the world. His concert in Boston was sold out with the average person paying a hundred dollars for their ticket. Two days before the performance he found a spot on the street with his violin worth three and a half million dollars and played intricate music by Bach for forty-five minutes. Yet, over a thousand people passed by without paying much attention.[39] We're compelled to stick with our first impression, seeing and treating people according to the initial value assessment. It derails our judgment when in a different context we would know better.

It goes the other way too. We unconsciously tend to value things according to what we paid for them. Like the aunt who goes to the thrift store to find a teacup for her eight-year-old niece's tea party. She finds a vintage-looking one she thinks her niece would like and buys it—after all, if it breaks, she's only lost a dollar. Years later she discovers it is an antique worth hundreds.

If you recognize any of these thoughts, your perception of value might be sabotaging your crossroads progress:

I have to keep my costs low because clients will only pay the lowest price.

This program is longer, so it must offer more valuable content.

Diagnosis or **confirmation bias** blinds us to evidence that contradicts our first impression. All it takes is a label or an insinuation to colour our perception.[40]

One study was done with an economics class, which had a substitute teacher for the day. Before the professor came in, the students were all given a bio outlining his qualifications and presentation style, except in half the bios there was a one-word difference. In one half he was described as a "warm person, industrious, critical, practical, and determined." In the other half he was described as a "cold person, industrious, critical, practical, and determined." After the professor taught the class, the students were given identical evaluations to fill out. Most of the students who received the bio describing him as "warm" used positive words in their review. The majority of the students who received the bio with the word "cold" didn't connect with him as well and used negative words in their questionnaire.[41]

At your crossroads you might recognize confirmation bias if you hear yourself saying:

"All the signs point to _____."

"I've always thought _____, and this experience proves it."

It's sobering to think maybe we're not as rational as we think we are.

If you're a perfectionist driven to do everything just right, this news might terrify you. But it also can be freeing. How liberating would it be to know there's another way to see things at your crossroads?

Dare to Be Real about What's Colouring Your Decision

What assumptions are you making about your options? What is your next step in adjusting those assumptions?

25

CREATING AN ENVIRONMENT FOR MAKING YOUR BEST DECISION

"The best asset we have for making a contribution to the world is ourselves. If we underinvest in ourselves, and by that I mean our minds, our bodies, and our spirits, we damage the very tool we need to make our highest contribution."

—Greg McKeown, *Essentialism: The Disciplined Pursuit of Less*

ark Zuckerberg, Facebook founder, wears a similar outfit every day. Leadership mentor Michael Hyatt sets out his running clothes every night and gets up at 5:30 a.m. to run. Minimalist mom and podcaster Allie Casazza regularly declutters her home, schedule, and life.[42] These successful influencers have adopted habits that maximize their energy for decision-making.

Before going on an out-of-town road trip, you probably fill up your gas tank. Maybe you've got a stash of trail mix ready too. Decision-making requires fuel as well. Each day, if you've had a decent sleep and nourished your body and soul the night before, you can wake up each morning filled up. Ideally, you're loaded with all sorts of yummy soul nutrients. Hope. Love. Energy. Wisdom. Purpose. Peace. Openness. Everything you need to meet the demands of the day.

Okay, maybe most days.

From that moment on, every choice you make draws on your inner resources. Each encounter with suffering depletes a little of your creativity, willpower, and stamina.

The term for this growing phenomenon is decision fatigue.

What made me pay attention to decision fatigue was a study done on judges making parole rulings.[43] These judges were experienced, educated people we trust to make deliberative evaluations. But this study discovered other factors might tamper with their decision process. After all, they are human. The researchers of this study documented the kinds of rulings they made over a few weeks as well as the time of sessions and breaks. To keep it scientific, they included some other controlling factors.

What did they discover?

Let's just say I would not want to be the person hoping for parole if their hearing was before the judge's lunch break. The likelihood of a favourable ruling was greater at the beginning of the workday and right after a break with food. It decreased to zero later into the session before the judge would take a break. Bottom line: our physiological state has a significant impact on our decisions.

Other studies discovered air quality, a full bladder, posture, distraction levels, numbers of options, and much more can affect your ability to make little choices or weighty decisions.

Here are ways you can create an ideal internal and external environment for your best decision.

Take re-energizing breaks throughout your day.

Research mentions a variety of ways to restore your energy: viewing scenes of nature, going for a walk, getting fresh air, taking a short rest, being around someone in a good mood, and having a snack. That wasn't news to me, but sometimes I need the reminder. I love concentrating intensely on a project and pushing through until it's finished. But if I don't take breaks and walk around a bit, even get some fresh air, I'll eventually hit a wall and have no inspiration to finish it. Other times I set time aside to write, but I feel irritable. I'd rather push through, but I've learned if I hit the highway for twenty minutes, go for a walk around the block, or tidy my desk, it gives my mind breathing room. What are ways you can make sure you're revitalized enough?

**Make important decisions earlier in
the morning or after a break.**

The timing of your decision matters. My parents had an agreement that they wouldn't have any important conversations to do any major decision-making before 9 a.m. (when my mom's mind woke up) or after 9 p.m. (when my dad's brain shut down). Some studies found the most popular decision-making days for nine-to-five-ers tend to be on Tuesdays or Wednesdays. While these might not relate to your rhythm of life, it's worth considering and giving yourself grace. When do you feel the most upbeat in the day? When do you feel the slump?

**Jump up and down for a minute,
dance, or sing to some music.**

I never imagined I would spend four twelve-hour days jumping up and down in a Tony Robbins conference. Once I did, I couldn't deny that changing my body's state makes a difference in my mental clarity, memory, and readiness to tackle what's ahead. Now, when my family is feeling sluggish in the morning, we turn on some music and have a dance party for five minutes before we go on with our day.

Simplify what you handle each day.
Gadgets are fun. They're supposed to save us time. But they can also be one more thing to fix or clean up in your day, draining you of the mental and emotional resources you need to prepare a better future. On the other hand, fixing something when you have the time might also help you to forget about what's weighing on you. In the process you might come up with inspiration. So, the next time you have to fix an appliance or clean up a workspace before you can move on with a project, consider this: would doing it now deplete or replenish your fuel for the day's decisions?

> Would doing this task now deplete or replenish your fuel for the day's decisions?

Create a preplanned routine for repetitive tasks every day or week.
Set out exercise clothes the night before. Order a meal kit to be delivered to your door on your busy days. Wear the same outfits on certain days. Eat the same thing for breakfast every day if you couldn't care less about food. Many moms order their groceries online because it saves their sanity. By avoiding shopping with their kids, they spend less money and maintain willpower by not letting impulsiveness sidetrack them.

Give yourself grace.
The thing is, your gumption and willpower aren't things you can conjure up on demand. They have ebbs and flows. The more we become aware of them, the more we can manage them with intentionality. If you're too hard on yourself, you will derail yourself. Grace frees you to do better.

Choose the best next step.

Sometimes the best decision is simply to make any decision. But if we believe our only option is to say yes or no to the big dream, we sink back into overwhelm. Thankfully, you don't have to tackle your big goal right now. It helps to break up the journey into milestones. Be kind to your brain and give yourself a timeline of baby steps to follow.

Create urgency.

Deadlines naturally force us to make a decision. For those of us who are prone to indecision and overthinking, we can often cop out and let the decision be made for us or spiral down into negativity and analysis paralysis. This ends up feeding a helplessness mindset and even resentment if we don't own the choice. We long for the perfect path to jump out and wave at us, but even if we recognize it, we've gotten too bogged down in our doubts to take the action we need to.

Dan Miller, career coach, author, and podcaster, says he gives himself two weeks to make any major decision because any more time only wastes energy for actually implementing the decision.[44] That approach might not work in your case, but what other kinds of timelines are available to you? Maybe your overthinking is lengthening your decision process, and you would find it helpful to give yourself an hour a day to journal. This will allow you to process the decision instead of letting it consume you all day. Once the hour is over, you free your mind and emotions for the other essential decisions in the day.

Maybe your crossroads comes with an application deadline, and you need to fast-track your decision-making process—whether it's for a job, a personal development opportunity, or going back to school. Applying is only one stage of the decision process. You can decide to say yes to phase one, knowing the step will bring clarity for a more confident yes or no at the next phase's deadline.

What if there isn't an external deadline? Except for the regret of missed opportunity, nothing is forcing you to make a decision. In that case you might need to increase your own urgency. The first draft of this book was taking forever to finish, and I kept pressing snooze on my writing times. At a dinner with other writers, we made ninety-day commitments of what we would have done the next time we met. I wrote down that I would have the second draft of my book done. That increased my urgency to get my first draft finished, but it still wasn't enough to push past my blocks.

Finally, I envisioned the moment I would have to confess at the next dinner that I didn't even get my first draft finished. I mapped out on my calendar what I would need to complete each week. Then, I reached out to a friend who I thought would give direct, enthusiastic feedback on my first draft. When she said yes to my deadline, my urgency amped up tenfold.

For some people, setting a date on a calendar works. ("I will make this decision by . . .") For others, an arbitrary deadline holds no motivation if there's no external cost, accountability, or reward. Making a commitment to someone who was excited about my goal was the motivation I needed. Whatever works for you—avoidance of pain or anticipation of something delightful—you don't have to rely on willpower alone to choose your next path.

Practical ways to create urgency for making this decision:

- Brainstorm all the pieces of your decision-making process. Jot down the dates involved, then enter them in your calendar.

- Choose a deadline for picking your crossroads path once you have the necessary information or related work completed.

- Invite accountability from a respected friend or mentor.

- Take some time to envision and journal what the cost will be in your life if you don't own this decision and make a shift. Then, write out what the outcome and reward would be on the other side of this decision.

- Create a consequence, cost, or reward high enough to kick your butt into gear and make sure you commit to your decision deadline.

Dare to Create the Environment for Your Best Decision

What environment do you need to choose your better future? Urgency? Peace? Grace to mess up? A baby step? A flow zone? A simplified daily routine? Fresh air?

26

DARE TO DECIDE:
Phases of Decision

"In light of my past experience . . . and my future hopes and dreams, what is the wise thing to do?"

—Andy Stanley

Change was in the wind.

My divorce papers had arrived months ago, and I was relieved the "I'm-married-but-I'm-not" years of my life were over. I felt at home in my new living arrangement, and I accepted that buying a house wouldn't happen any time soon. Many friendships shifted as one by one, singles in my former group married off. I was now co-leading a different small group of people as part of a new initiative, and I enjoyed sorting out the new dynamics. My writing critique group was still the highlight of my week though my novel-writing only puttered along.

It felt as if life had settled into a pleasant groove.

Now what, God? I asked, sitting in my car, looking over the grey waters of Lake Ontario.

For years I had tracked my life in phases of growth. The seasons of surviving a marriage breakdown, healing from rejection, believing in my potential, growing in leadership, and pursuing my house dream had been grueling. Now that I saw how resilient I had become, it felt satisfying—but those seasons were hard. I sensed a new season of growth would be coming soon.

My other dreams were in motion or shelved, but one sat hidden. I still wanted to have a family one day. Since I was in my thirties, I figured I should do something about it. But that meant facing the fate of dating.

Ugh.

Hanging out places where you might find a healthy-minded guy whose company you might enjoy, making time to go on dates with strangers, navigating hidden expectations—after hearing my single friends' woes, it all sounded exhausting and exasperating. The summer after my marriage ended, I read a pile of books, and one takeaway stuck with me: truly healing from rejection comes through being in a relationship and learning to trust someone reliable. While I would have preferred to pre-learn that lesson on my own in a context I controlled, it doesn't work that way.

"At some point I know I'm going to have to face this," I told God aloud. "I would like to get married and have kids one day. So, if you want my next season to be about dating and healing that rejection wound, I'm game. But I'm still getting my energy back. Could we make it a *fun* growing season this time?"

Then, just so God knew what He had to work with, I launched into my dare. "I have no idea how you're going to accomplish this. I'm not going online—I spend enough time on the computer for work and writing. My life is packed with things important to me, so I don't even know where You're going to fit dating into my life. But if you want to this to be my next season of growth, go for it."

I couldn't help chuckling at myself for giving God my terms. He would do what He felt best. But my life finally was stabilized, and I didn't want to upset that. At peace with trusting Him, I figured I would let Him sort all that out.

My first couple of dating experiences had more to do with God's sense of humour than getting to know someone. Then, within a year of my prayer, a cute, quiet tech guy showed up in my life.

While it took shy James another year to talk to me, he somehow made it through my coworkers' ploys to set us up and the confusing experience of dating me. We went on magical nighttime hikes in fresh snow, clomped through muddy excursions that made us want to cry, and traversed through awkward conversations. As I enjoyed the heart-pattering moments of feeling special again, I wrestled through tempering my fear and trusting him.

My dating story is far from formulaic. Every person's story is different, full of its own themes. I had found peace and fulfillment in singleness, and this new season was nerve-wracking. Had I not decided to invite God to make this a fun adventure, my skittishness probably would have made me bail before saying, "I do."

LET'S GO SLOW

Decisive go-getters who make quick decisions can frustrate me because they go through the phases of decision seamlessly. I appreciate their energy to move forward, but often their advice comes out as "just make the decision" when they try to help someone else. It sounds so simple. But what about when options seem complicated? How can you be objective when fear is having a heyday? If I'm stuck in overwhelm, or if I simply need time to process the implications, a comment like "just make a decision" sends me into panicked paralysis topped with shame for not being able to decide faster.

Your reasons for holding back are sensible to you. So, how can you accept the dare to decide wholeheartedly, even in uncertainty? It helped me to slow this way down like a slow-mo replay inspection of the three phases of decision.

1. Lean In

Like test-driving a car or selecting clothes to try on in the change room, first you can take time to lean into your preferred option. Set a time limit and try the option for a few hours or days. Imagine the outcome. The more you can visualize it, the more your mind knows what it's after, and it will work on your behalf consciously and unconsciously. Check in with the people this option would impact. Test it as a hypothesis. Observe what you see, sense, and hear. Get a house inspection on the house you want to buy. Shadow someone in the field you're considering for a career change. Weigh the pros and cons. Chart the data you've collected.

This isn't the time to let fear call the shots. Believe wholeheartedly for a while that this is what you want or that this could work. Then weigh in. If you gave it a serious try, is it working? Even if it doesn't work out the way you expect, how could failure still get you farther ahead in some way? What would you need to tweak?

Each time I hung out with James, I had to evaluate what I saw in his character. Were the things drawing me to him healthy, or was it a past pattern from unhealthy relationships? We had to hash it out in some uncomfortable conversations.

After a trial period ends, it's time to call the verdict. Is this still the preferred option, or is it time to try out another?

2. Decide

How do you know if you've really decided to go back to school, write a book, or register for a triathlon? Do you feel a certain amount of resolve? Do you write it down? Tell someone? Pay someone? Call the media? Write a social post? Put it on the calendar? Making the decision requires some kind of action. In my adventure to begin dating again, I actually had to go out with a guy when the opportunity arose. Then I had to decide if the relationship was worth moving from friendship to commitment. One night under an umbrella, with the sound of waves and rain surrounding us, I said, "Yes, I'll marry you," and accepted a ring with a sparkling solitaire.

If your life were a story, you could call the decision at your crossroads an inciting incident. It's a point in the story when something happens that disrupts everyday life and tosses the character into the story—no going back.

In his book *A Million Miles in a Thousand Years*, Donald Miller talks about what he learned from a renowned screenwriting expert while Don was figuring out how to edit his life. "Robert McKee says humans naturally seek comfort and stability. Without an inciting incident that disrupts their comfort, they won't enter into a story. They have to get fired from their job or be forced to sign up for a marathon. A ring has to be purchased. A home has to be sold. The character has to jump into the story, into the discomfort and the fear, otherwise the story will never happen."[45] The more he understood this, the more he applied it to his own life. He began to live with more intentionality, even if that meant signing up for a cross-country bicycle ride to raise money to build wells in third world countries. (He and gym equipment weren't on good terms back then.)

Once you settle on a preferred path, intention and faith aren't enough to move you forward. As I observe the difference between people who jump in and go for what they want and those who stay cautiously on the sidelines, I notice something.

The more decisive they are, the more often they take immediate action. Thus, the more they seem to get out of life.

Do they make mistakes? Yep. Do they have to make course corrections? Sure, they do. But they choose to learn from what they experienced, and they use that wisdom to make their next decision. After weighing what they want and what they need to know, they move forward with their best next action for the moment. They let hope dictate their choices rather than fear.

Have you ever noticed fear and excitement sometimes feel the same?

If you've been spending most of your crossroads time overwhelmed by fear, what if you've mistaken your excitement for fear? Give yourself permission to enjoy accepting your call into this new adventure.

3. Release

Another mistake that keeps us stuck at our crossroads comes at this last phase. Choosing a path means letting go of where you've been. When you say yes to one direction, that means you're saying yes to learning the skills and investing the time, energy, and focus that path requires. It also means you'll be saying no to other paths. After living in limbo for so long, losing this familiarity feels especially hard. You get comfortable with the options, people, and commitments you would have to leave behind, so even if you're ready to move forward, the emotions that well up can surprise you.

Most people I talk to look for a sign they've made the right decision before they move into the release stage. Usually, the sign they look for is peace or relief. Other times, their confidence comes from an epiphany. But I haven't always found that's the case, and I was relieved to hear I wasn't the only one when my friend Anna Fransden told me her story.

Anna is a business coach and mentor for online female entrepreneurs. I was drawn to her gentle, optimistic, and integral approach in helping heart-centered women. As I watched her grow her Facebook group to six thousand and fully book her group programs within her first two years as a coach, I had no idea the turmoil she was feeling behind the scenes.

She started out as a therapist at a college where her clients came into her office struggling with mental issues and sub-optimal health. Her role was to bring them to basic health, then nudge them back on their own so they wouldn't become dependent on her. After a few years of this, Anna craved taking clients to a level where they could thrive. Finally, her husband encouraged her to try something different, so she offered a local life coaching workshop. She fell in love with coaching.

"Actually, I felt like a con artist taking people's money because it felt so easy and enjoyable," Anna says in her live videos to her online tribe.

After her first taste of life coaching, Anna opened an online Facebook group, and it grew—much to her delight. Soon she was offering online life coaching programs and helping women grow their online businesses. That brought her to her first major crossroads. Now she was balancing life coaching, business coaching, and therapy. Knowing she could only handle two major focuses well at a time, she had to give one up. Loyal to a fault, she sat on the fence for months, torn between everything she cared about. Finally, she chose to release life coaching.

Being pregnant brought her to another major crossroads later that year. Soon she would be juggling three things: a baby, her therapy client load, and her business coaching. If she could only handle two major things well, she would have to let go of one job.

"How did that feel?" I asked when she shared her story with me on a phone call.

"I felt so much pressure to make the perfect decision. It was awful," she groaned. "Really crappy. It felt like the world was ending."

Anna's husband and her coach, both knowing her desires and strengths, encouraged her to give up her therapy job.

They challenged her reasoning and called her out on the way she was dealing with it.

Still, every day in both her therapy and her coaching client sessions she had moments where she felt, "I was born for this!" Her role at the college was a really good position, holding the security of a paycheck and an environment she enjoyed. Yet, her coaching business had room for expansion, and she loved the results her clients were experiencing. She would be letting go of something good for a more desirable option, but that didn't make her feel better about it. How could she choose?

Finally, Anna decided to give up her therapy practice. She knew it was the right decision, but it didn't feel good. Actually, she wanted to throw up. It felt complicated and weird.

Relief didn't come till much later.

When you're feeling torn about a decision, it's tempting to hold onto a back-up plan. While it's true some plans are reversable (if you move away, you can always move back) in most cases, tentatively trying out your plan will give you a very different experience than fully committing. An aerialist's life is on the line if they don't fully commit to the leap from one trapeze to another. Saying "I do" to James meant any other guy out there was no longer an option if I wanted a healthy marriage. Even how I spent my time changed when I got married. Had I tried to hold on to all my relationships the same as I did when I was single, they all would have suffered. Then, when our daughter was born the following year, a whole new adventure began. There was no going back.

When you release the options and decide you're giving a new direction your all, you treat it much differently. Tenacity kicks in. Your strength and focus are freed up to invest in this new direction because you're not looking back. Failure doesn't even have to be a factor because you know you can count on it as a learning experience.

ENOUGH TO DARE

So, how can you trust you've gathered enough information to make your decision?

The year I experienced my "This is it!" epiphanies in discovering my love for purpose discovery and coaching, I was ready for my next steps. I only wasn't sure what those were . . . until I learned about transformational leadership coaching training. I signed up. That season, going through the training, I felt my soul leap many times.

This is what I was meant for!

Still, under the surface shame taunted me, and inferiority made me doubt that this could be my thing.

Who was I to think this admin girl who hid behind a computer all day could help people surpass their self-imposed limits? I was only starting to surpass my own limits. How could I dare to help others do the same?

One day, as I was writing notes from my textbook, a Bible verse leapt out to me.

"Everything we could ever need for life and complete devotion to God has already been deposited in us by his divine power. For all this was lavished upon us through the rich experience of knowing him who has called us by name and invited us to come to him through a glorious manifestation of his goodness."

— 2 Peter 1:3 (TPT)

First, this verse spoke to the codependency and unrealistic expectations I regretted from past relationships. Instead of believing people were capable and responsible for handling their own lives, I tried to better their lives by sacrificing myself, controlling, and worrying. I did not only need better boundaries. Had I truly believed they had access to everything they needed to live up to their potential, I could have inspired them to own their lives better instead of trying to advise them how I thought they should live.

Once that revelation hit me, I felt a sense of relief. The verse became even more personal.

I have that belief in you, I sensed Jesus say. *I have given you everything you need: passion. Taste for what else is out there for you. Your calming gift of being present and compassionate. Training opportunities. Enough provision and time to take your next step. The supportive relationships of people who believe in you. You have access to My divine power so you don't have to do this on your own.*

You have all this because you have gotten to know Me and become more like Me. And through this impact you'll help others experience My goodness by believing in their potential when they don't yet.

Tears of awe blurred the pages of my journal. I felt the freedom of new confidence.

Did that mean I wasn't indecisive or insecure anymore? Nope. But when I found myself floundering at crossroads, waiting for certainty, that verse became my mantra. It fueled my courage to "Ready or not—act!" It trained me to trust my process, including my dating adventure, and then decide.

When the scenes in your life aren't moving your story forward, scrounging for more tips, ideas, and affirmation will only circle back to the same conflicting or incomplete information. It's time to remind yourself of everything you already have to start your new adventure.

- Your character—the person you've chosen to be through this process

- Ability to relinquish what you can't control through the power of surrender

- An honest inventory of your dreams and desires

- Flexibility to set a timeline for this decision

- Path options, even if they're imperfect or uncertain

- A collection of facts, identified feelings, and their signals

- Input from God and Dare to Decide friends

- Ability to evaluate your path options through the filter of your purpose, principles, and priorities

Now it's time to trust what you have been given and call the decision.

The Latin word for "decide" literally means to "cut off." Think about other words that have the suffix "cide." Genocide. Homicide. Suicide. Pesticide. Germicide. In each of those words something dies.[46] That means you need to start lopping off options at some point so you're free to move forward unhindered, unreservedly.

The weariness of waiting for a perfect decision is stealing the energy you need to live your story. At some point, logic, pep talks, and perfect answers won't give you clarity. Your brain will keep cycling through all the options as long as they're on the table.

Clarity peaks through the fog as you eliminate options, lean toward your preference, and try it out. Clarity shines brighter with more decisive action.

Dare to Decide

At what part of the decision process do you stall out? What could help you move forward?

27

CASE STUDY:
To Quit or Stay?

*"A waiting person is a patient person. The word
patience means the willingness to stay where we are
and live the situation out to the full in the belief that
something hidden there will manifest itself to us."*

—Henri J.M. Nouwen

What if your hard decision is to stay when you would rather go? To stay in the job that's making you miserable or boring you to tears? Staying in the career a few years longer because of your pension payout? Continuing to care for the elderly parents who need you, or your young kids, when you ache for the satisfaction of a career? Staying in your town because you want your kids to grow up around their grandparents when you long to live in a different climate or explore a new adventure? It would be heaven not to deal with that workload, that stress, that manager, that schedule anymore and start fresh. Sometimes the hardest crossroads decision is to stay instead of go, even if it's only for a season.

My dad modelled this for me when I was growing up.

He faced the same question every teen does when he was growing up in Southern Ontario, Canada: what career do I want to have when I grow up? Anything to do with English was out—he hated creative writing and grammar. But what he loved was outdoors activities such as hunting, birdwatching, and canoeing. When he wasn't outdoors, he was working with wood—making a canoe or crafting furniture. He also discovered a love for art—sketching, painting, carving soap stone. So, he looked at career avenues that would let him do some of those things.

As he considered designing his life's direction, he knew two other factors were nonnegotiable to him: faith and family. As one of eight kids raised in a Dutch family, having a family one day and providing for them was important to him. So was staying active in his faith. Art wasn't guaranteed to pay well, so that didn't seem like a smart path. Plus, he liked the idea of keeping something he enjoyed as a hobby. Construction paid well, but he wasn't a fan of the lifestyle. That left a career in the outdoors. Not long after he joined the Junior Rangers program, Dad knew he was on a track he loved. That led to attending a university for a degree in forestry.

After four years of education in northern Ontario, now with a wife and two daughters (one being me), it was time for him to find a job. He had no idea where. At the time, the trees—and the jobs—were in Northern Ontario and BC. Cold, snowy, somewhat isolated, and small-townish, Ontario had a surplus of applicants from which employers could take their pick. He heard British Columbia had a shortage of forestry workers, and some of his classmates were getting hired there.

The rugged coastal terrain and mild weather beckoned him. But with temporary contracts, no benefits, no seniority, and the stress of wondering if he would be re-hired every March, it was risky. Not to mention his family would have to live in a mobile home while they were there. Nevertheless, he and my mom packed up the contents of their tiny apartment and drove our family across the four provinces. When they reached the glorious Rocky Mountains, Dad's awe compelled him to steer with one hand, snapping photos with the other as the windy roads took them along rivers and railways, through tunnels and passes, and up steep inclines. The Trans-Canada took them along the seething Fraser River, with jagged rocks bordering one side of the road, to canyon drop-offs mere feet from the others side. In Vancouver they met the Pacific Ocean. A ferry threaded its way between evergreen-saturated islands until they reached Vancouver Island.

The first year working in the rugged, isolated terrain of the island, he couldn't believe the job he accepted. It was wonderful getting to enjoy everything he loved doing. And here, while the places where he worked were remote, the family could live in a bigger city. There was something about a town with a Walmart that seemed like a desirable place to raise a family.

Year after year his contract was renewed. Every month he would spend a week bunking in a tiny trailer, riding a dirt bike along muddy logging roads, and taking a motorboat to secluded islands to check on logging sites. The rest of the month, back in the office he worked out ideas to solve problems or make methods better.

"What did you learn about yourself back then?" I asked Dad when he was telling me about these early days.

"In those days the government employees' way was to turn their brain off at lunch. But I realized as an introvert my best ideas happen in my off time. So, I ignored all that and worked through my lunch whenever I wanted. Or at two in the morning, I would wake up with an idea, get up, and sketch it out. Early in my career I looked at what everyone else was doing and following, then said, 'The heck with that.'"[47]

He managed to stay in the technical field, outside corporate politics, for years. But by the time the sixth child was born, Mom wasn't keen on managing the family on her own for a week every month. Dad went through an interview process that positioned him in a professional and supervisory capacity with more pay in a new city off the island.

The new position turned out to be absolutely fabulous. He could implement a bunch of ideas he had tested out on the island. He would simply look for complaints that something wasn't working and implement his ideas. Some worked, and others didn't.

As a teen by that time, I didn't know any of this. All I knew was that Dad went to work every day, came home, kissed my mom (who was making dinner in the kitchen), and then disappeared into his woodworking shop to decompress. I never knew how much he loved his job all those years. He was just Dad, going to work like an adult is supposed to. Though some days were stressful, Dad wasn't the type to complain to us kids, so I figured that was merely part of life. That adults somehow knew how to put in their time and keep going.

I didn't realize how tense team dynamics were getting for him at the office until I overheard him mention he had gone to our pastor for advice about whether to quit or stay in his job.

That jarred me.

Dad wasn't happy at his job? Dad's job was our security. The years of dedication in a government job and their wisdom with money allowed Mom to stay with the kids and homeschool us. He intentionally chose a position that gave us the predictability of him being home every evening. It gave him five weeks of vacation time that let us go camping in the summer or spend weeks driving to and from Ontario to visit family or see the redwood forests of California and the Grand Canyon.

The thought of Dad being so stressed and unhappy in his job that he would quit was sobering to my sense of stability and my compassion. That's when I started paying attention over the years to what was getting him so stressed: an overbearing management style that left him and his team seething or deflated.

Even telling me about it years later, Dad was too respectful of others to say many details. But he let it be known he was ready to quit. That got the attention of his direct report and the superior. They pulled him aside to find out what was wrong and offered an explanation about the management approach.

"You're too valuable to this team. We can't accept your resignation," they told him.

That was a turning point for Dad. If he couldn't change them, the only person he could change was himself. *I can interpret this negatively, or I can see it objectively and find a way to respond differently,* he thought.

> Each path, each choice, comes with its own treasures.

The biggest revelation came through reading a book on leadership. It showed him options of how he could respond to different situations, and he was astonished. *"You mean I can respond* that *way? I've only been doing it* this *way!"*

With his new toolbox of perspectives and skills, he changed. His team noticed a difference and started commenting.

"How'd you take all that?" they would ask after a grueling meeting.[48]

"Now, I just respond differently," Dad told them. "I emotionally remove myself from the situation and see myself as a third person in the room, listening. Then, I coach myself on how to respond."

Soon he began advising them on how to respond in situations they dreaded.

He pushed himself to participate in meetings to keep communication open, even if he didn't have anything to say. The more he stepped back in the conversations to see it objectively, the more grace he had for the people involved. He realized the management was only trying their best to express themselves the only way they knew how.

The worst of the season happened over a couple years, but Dad spent the rest of his years applying what he had learned. He earned a lot of respect because of it. After thirty years in forestry, he retired only to become a sought-after consultant. Contractors found his experience, his approach to problem-solving, and the skills he used in conflict management indispensable for navigating government forestry permits and regulations.

I have often wished my crossroads made more sense at the time or that paths revealed themselves earlier. I wanted the path that came with the least amount of suffering.

But every path has its hardships, whether you stay or leave, whether you finish or start something. And each path, each choice, comes with its own treasures. How it shapes you. The new lens through which you see opportunities. New dreams that excite you.

The sooner you choose a path and wholeheartedly surrender to the journey, the sooner you will experience the fullness of what that path has to offer, whether it's to stay a season longer or embrace a new adventure.

Dare to Discern

What's another approach you could take towards your hard decision? What could you read, or who could you talk with to see your situation differently?

PART VI

THE JOURNEY

28

CREATING YOUR NEW NORMAL

*"The man who moves a mountain begins
by carrying away small stones."*

—Confucius

"I s your daughter in school yet?" asked a friend whom I hadn't seen in a while.

"Yes, she's in junior kindergarten at Calvary," I replied.

"Oh, she must be with Donna Jo, then."

"Yes! We love her."

My friend shook her head in admiration. "That is one special lady. She had such a way with our daughter when she was in her class. We're so grateful."

I wholeheartedly agreed. "She has a calling for sure."

That's about how the conversation went anytime Donna Jo's name was mentioned. Wonderment, admiration, and sometimes teary gratitude saturated those ten-second conversations. Donna Jo and her dear team ran the most loving, orderly, peaceful class of twenty-three three-, four-, and five-year-olds I'd ever seen. Through her kindness, the fun songs and stories she taught, and the moments she nurtured wholesome character, those kids knew they were loved. When I'm in her presence, I feel refreshed, hopeful, and known. There's something attractive about someone who is delightfully grounded in who she is and what she's called to do. When my daughter came home from school, giddy to tell me about the story of Esther or a new "character word" she learned, I sensed it. When Donna Jo came into the church office to make arrangements for the funeral of her mom, who she adored, I felt it. When I pass by her in the church lobby and her face lights up with a genuine smile, I feel it.

Is she naturally like that? Or are there things she does to become like that, things you and I can do to achieve that same peace-filled, vibrant presence?

Though Donna Jo and I accidentally found out we're second cousins, it wasn't until ten years later when we met over coffee to plan a retreat breakout session we were leading together that I heard her story. That's when I had a better understanding of why she is who she is today.

Though she had wanted to be a teacher when she was young, after college and marriage she started out as a stay-at-home mom, pouring care into her kids, running a home daycare, and even homeschooling. She never imagined the impact she would have on hundreds of families over the years. Then, one day her life changed. She had just stopped by a private Christian school because she heard their library was available to homeschoolers. As she walked by the classrooms, something leaped in her heart, and she knew she wanted her kids to experience this.[49]

She went home and told her husband.

"That's impossible! We have no money for that!" With her husband going back to college for a new degree, private school was not in the budget.

But Donna Jo knew what was in her heart and trusted God would show her the way.

That September, on the day her kids arrived in their grades three and five classrooms for the first time, she also started her position there as a part-time kindergarten teacher. She had no doubt God had lined up opportunities at exactly the right time, and she continued to see His provisions year after year. She rarely knew her next step when she stepped into a new course or role.

When the school included three-year-olds in their preschool program, she was the one person on staff who already had the mandated credentials.

When the principal asked her to be part of a special education team and take an intense course load on educating children with autism and other exceptionalities, her first response was, "Sure, I'll do it, but that's not really my thing." After pouring herself into her studies, not only did she come away with a certification she didn't expect, but it opened the door to invitations to speak at teacher conferences.

When the school approved her to be vice principal, she realized she had already been prepared for the position.

As she accepted and thrived in her new role, it became a part of who she was. It expanded how she lived her purpose, even though she never planned for it or expected it. She loved her life.

She also thrived on helping people. When her mom found out she had cancer, though the thought of losing her was scary, Donna Jo fully embraced bringing her to appointments, shopping for her, and taking care of her. Her parents were living in the basement suite, and it was her greatest joy to spend an hour with her mom over coffee at the beginning of her day, sharing what was on her heart. They believed for healing and did everything they could to bring her to the road to recovery, yet when it was clear her mom's life was nearing an end, Donna Jo still trusted God and accepted how things were turning out.

After her mom's death, it wasn't long before life began to drag with no appointments, errands, or caregiving to fill her time. After showing up wholeheartedly in the best way she knew how, she wondered, *What's the reward for all that?* But all she was left with was grief and the task of creating a new normal.

Donna Jo took some time to recover from a surgery of her own, but when she returned to work, she felt worn. While she still enjoyed her role, she didn't feel the same energy and passion she used to.

It felt as if she was approaching a crossroads. Was it time to move on and find something new? This question was normally something she would have talked through with her mom. Sipping her coffee in the morning, never feeling more alone, she burst out (not for the first time), "Okay, now I want her back! I did it, God. I did everything You asked me to do. I gave her up, I let her go, I accepted Your plan. Now, I want her back! I want to have coffee with her like I used to every morning."[50]

On that morning she felt a strong tug on her heart.

Well, I would like to have coffee with you in the morning. I would like to hear about the good things and bad things going on. I would like to be that person in your life, she sensed God say.

At that moment Donna Jo realized that in many areas of her life, she had made her mom her source instead of God. She'd had a special space in her day where someone fed into her heart and soul, but it wasn't supposed to be her mom.

Donna Jo curled her hand tighter around her mug, mulling over her new reality. "Okay, so this is my new normal. I sit with You in the morning and tell You all the good things that are happening and the awful things that are happening that You already know. And I'll be receiving from You what I would have gotten from her."

Early the next morning Donna Jo woke up before the rest of the household and turned on her coffeemaker. She had tried to do the good Christian thing and have regular devotion times with God before, but it never stuck. It felt forced, awkward. This time it would be different. If she and God were going to have a chat together over coffee, just like she and her mom had, that meant He wanted her to be fully herself. It meant that He'd be delighted in the little things that brought her joy. She showered so she would be awake and alert but then put her pajamas back on, still wanting to feel relaxed and cozy. Then, she settled in her favourite chair with all her favourite things: her mug of coffee, a comfy blanket, a brand-new journal, coloured pens, her Bible, and an old devotional book she found in the basement.

Drawing in a deep, contented breath, she opened the devotional.

Over the next few months this practice grew to be her favourite time of day. Nestled with coffee and a blanket in her favourite chair, she would read the simple devotional, look up the scripture for the day, and journal her feelings, observations, and questions with the brightly coloured pens.

She noticed God's presence filled her up in its own way, the same way being with her mom had filled her up. And while she still didn't have the same passion and energy for her job, the new morning rhythm did renew her hope.

STEP-BY-STEP FAITH TO EMERGING CLARITY

After you've been stuck at a crossroads for a while, you start longing for momentum. You want to feel alive with progress. You crave the satisfaction of accomplishing something. In your story you want to feel like each scene makes sense and moves towards something meaningful.

Life is filled with crossroads and Dare to Decide moments. Sometimes you know they're significant. You're not sure how it's all going to come together, but you're filled with curious faith. Other times, we don't realize their significance until later. Then there are times when life stalls to a halt and yet keeps going at the same time, such as when my first husband left or when Donna Jo's mom died, or a pandemic changes life as you knew it. Life isn't the same now, and you had no choice in the matter. What you want you can't have, so you're not even sure what to want anymore.

One thing is for sure. Whether you have a flicker of faith or mountains of it, only intentional action will move you out of a crossroads and into fresh clarity.

Remember Caroline Williams from chapter seven, who was on a mission to discover fresh purpose and a new career? She didn't know how her life would turn out. Her clarity emerged as she took one next best step at a time, such as daring to move to New York City to fulfill a bucket-list dream, joining yoga instructor training even though it didn't make sense, and sharing her journey on Instagram and YouTube.

For me, it was being faithful with the opportunities already in my life. Momentum didn't come because I went looking for it. It came through leaning into pain instead of avoiding it, trusting good can come from rotten situations, and using my gifts when I saw opportunities.

For Donna Jo to have deeper clarity and refreshed energy in her calling, she started with her new morning rhythm. She didn't know this would lead to a transforming encounter that would not only change her life but inspire hundreds of teachers and women.

Dare to Leave Your Crossroads

Think about what scares you most about life on the other side of your decision. What big action (or daily rhythm) do you think might help prepare you with the peace, insight, and energy for your new normal?

29

SMALL RHYTHMS, BIG MOMENTUM

The Lord is my shepherd, I lack nothing.
He makes me lie down in green pastures,
he leads me beside quiet waters,
he refreshes my soul.
He guides me along the right paths for his name's sake.
Even though I walk through the darkest valley,
I will fear no evil, for you are with me;
your rod and your staff, they comfort me.

—Psalm 23, (NIV)

T he room was packed with women around tables, listening to Donna Jo. She and I had prepared a retreat session together, and we were finally presenting it after all our hard work.[51] Each woman had a reason why they chose "From Stress to Purpose" as their breakout. Some were juggling a career, courses, and family life; others were recovering from postpartum; still others were worn out from the rat race. Donna Jo's part of the presentation was based on the revelation she received reading Psalm 23 during one of her early morning God times. She told me the story in the coffee shop when we discussed what we would cover in our breakout session, and the women were as riveted as I was.

After a few months of waking up early to spend time with God, she still didn't have the passion and energy she used to have in her work, but she had begun to notice a difference. On the days she had that coffee hour with God, she felt happier and more confident. She would be the first person to smile a greeting at a student, colleague, or parent, and that would set a positive tone for the whole conversation. But on the days she didn't, she felt more insecure and sensitive to looks or comments, making her second-guess herself.

The morning she opened her Bible to Psalm 23, the Shepherd's Psalm, God was waiting to show her a way she could find her joy and purpose again. And it had nothing to do with a new career.

Line by line, fresh insight flowed in coloured ink across the pages of her journal.

The Lord is my shepherd;
I shall not want.

If she truly believed that, she needed to fully yield to Him, just as she had when she said yes to teaching, accepted her mom's death, and spoke at teacher conferences. But what exactly did yielding mean now?

He makes me to lie down in green pastures.

Just as spending time with Jesus and His word every morning became her green pasture for spiritual nourishment, physical food was intended to nourish her body. It was time to take better care of herself, to eat for health rather than live only to eat.

He leads me beside the still waters.

A quote she had heard came back to her: "The solution to pollution is dilution." It held true both spiritually and physically. Her mind carried toxic thoughts every day. She had already felt the benefits of washing her spirit with the water of God's Word. But her body also carried toxins, and she knew she didn't drink enough water. She knew she needed to be refreshed with water before she drank anything else, and this would bring health both to her body and her mind.

As Donna Jo shared her story with the breakout group, some women filled their handouts with notes while others abandoned their handouts to listen intently.

"'He restores my soul,'" she said, quoting the next verse. "God wanted to heal my body, mind, and emotions. But to heal yesterday's wounds and prepare for today's challenges, I realized I needed time in His presence every day. God's grace is for today's reality, not for tomorrow's worries."

As she was about to move on to the next verse, a couple of the ladies stopped her. "Whoa! Say that again!"

"God's grace is for today's reality, not for tomorrow's worries." She paused as everyone stilled, letting those words sink in.[52]

Even I wrote down the line in my journal, mulling it over. How often did I worry about tomorrow's problems instead of making the most of today's opportunities?

Donna Jo wrapped up her talk with the last verse. "'And I will dwell in the house of the Lord forever.' Life is hard, but I was seeing that life wasn't just about the here and now. Suddenly, eternity mattered a whole lot more. Not only because I would see Mom again, but because in falling in love with Jesus in a new way, I know everything will be worth it when I see Him in heaven. God is enough in my struggles, and I can't wait for the day I hear him say, 'Well done, My good and faithful servant.' This gave me a renewed purpose in what

God had called me to now. In order to fulfill that calling, I had to care for the body, mind, and time God entrusted to me."

The quiet women and their serious faces told me their minds were full, and I was glad we had included a reflection time on our agenda. I needed it too before walking everyone through the practical exercises.

What inspired me most about Donna Jo's story was that she was living it. After her spiritual download, she made sure she drank three bottles of water before having her beloved coffee during her morning break. She joined a clean eating challenge to teach herself what kind of food her body needed. She accepted a friend's invitation to join a gym, and though she doesn't always feel like going, she doesn't consider her day finished until she's gone for her workout after supper.

I could relate more to her in the days before she started her morning time with God, starting and lapsing in habits I knew were good for me. Many of the rhythms that will give you energy are things you already know to do. But when it's something we see as optional, that's often not motivating enough to establish those disciplines. However, when we can directly tie our rhythms to the process of becoming the person we want to be, we feel more inspired.

RHYTHMS THAT BUILD MOMENTUM

Before your habits become habits and your routines become routines, they're often muddled attempts of training your mind, body, and will to do things at regular times. Some days you do it because you want to. But on the days when you don't feel like it, it's a battle. Creating new rhythms naturally means you'll encounter resistance. Just like riding a bike, the first few pushes of the pedal are going to be the toughest. It also rubs against the expectations of others. Getting up early didn't go well with my young daughter when she looks forward to our snuggle time in the morning. Eating healthier doesn't always have positive reactions from your family members. But the more you fall into rhythms, the more it becomes ingrained in your life. And then, your friends and family not only expect it of you, they might start holding you to it.

Once you dare to choose your path and leave behind the other options, intentional action moves you forward.

You might be tempted to reorganize your whole life and plan out all your steps. But more often I hear from people who made substantial shifts in their life that clarity comes when one specific action turns into a rhythm. Like Caroline going to yoga regularly, my dad writing down ideas when they came to him, and Donna Jo having her God time early every morning.

> Your movement forward will come with consistent actions. These rhythms create space in your life, nurture what you expect of yourself, and hone your skills.

Maybe you started with one inciting incident such as signing up for a course or applying for a new job. Or perhaps it's a small step, such as planning a coffee meet-up with someone who's doing what you want to do. Nevertheless, your movement forward will come with consistent actions. These rhythms usually serve to create space in your life, nurture what you expect of yourself, and hone your skills. They become drops in the bucket of your potential that will one day be full to the brim.

Your action will probably look different than the next person's, but here are some of the rhythms that created momentum for others.

Drink Water
Start with something simple to tackle. I heard my whole life I was supposed to drink eight glasses of water a day. It wasn't until I heard Donna Jo's story that I noticed how I felt when I didn't drink enough water in a day. My brain would get foggy. When I came home from work, I would want to lay on the

couch and not get up. I started copying how others motivated themselves to drink enough water. Berries and peppermint leaves in their water. Carrying around water bottles—little ones and giant ones. Finally, I put an alarm on my phone. When it rings at my desk, in a team meeting, or in the car with my daughter, everyone in my life knows what it means and comments on it, giving me the accountability I appreciate (but never planned for).

Nutrition and Exercise

I'm one of those people who isn't a fan of sweating or exercise. And there are dozens of things I would rather do than figure out something healthy to make for meals. But what you put into your body makes a difference in your moods, your mental clarity, and your energy. I'm more motivated when I know others are doing it—often it doesn't even matter who. So, when I've lapsed and it's time to build rhythm again, I reconnect it to why it matters. (Examples: I want to set up my daughter for healthy habits; I want to be around as long as possible for her; I simply feel better afterwards and feeling better will help me work on my goals.) Then, I talk to others who are crushing it, and motivation rises.

Master Your Morning Ritual

I've had many morning routines in the last ten years. After being inspired by Donna Jo's story, I bought coloured pens and tried to journal my reflections on Bible verses every morning. But I had a one-year-old who somehow knew the moment I woke up, no matter the time. I read blogs about entrepreneurs who shared their morning rituals[53] and how that gave them momentum for their goals and dreams. After realizing everyone simply did what worked best for them, I gave myself grace to be flexible. One thing I knew for sure: having at least an hour of quiet morning time to myself is sacred to me. God help the person who intrudes on it too soon! In book-writing seasons, I would write in the mornings before doing anything else. In the winter, when my body would feel too stiff to write, I would put on one of Caroline's yoga videos or go for a walk first. If you need the inspiration for a morning rhythm that excites you, explore some links and ideas at daretodecide.ca/morningritual.

> **Find inspiration for your own morning rhythm at daretodecide.ca/morningritual.**

Welcome Stillness

It's easy to get caught in a cycle of achieving and crashing or plodding through life with no spark. Society expects us to be always on and current on all the latest news and trends. Noise bombards us from every direction, leaving us drained emotionally, mentally, and spiritually. It's no wonder sometimes you lose sight of your true self.

As a thinker I have always valued stillness. After a few people made comments accusing me of laziness, I started to feel guilty, even though Psalm 46:10 is one of my favourite verses: "Be still and know I am God." That guilt released after watching two high-achievers, Caroline Williams[54] and minimalist mama Allie Casazza,[55] talk about how they practice stillness. They took it to a whole new level, choosing to do nothing and think nothing for fifteen minutes a day. Not praying or reflecting, not planning or enduring. Just being. Observing the thoughts that come and go. It's certainly a humbling discipline to be still when there's a lot to do, but it's so worth it.

Practice Courage

At age twenty I sensed a call to move to St. Catharines, Ontario, a city where I'd never been, where I had no job and no car, and where I only knew one family. After that burst of courage, my boldness dwindled away. If I couldn't see a sensible step-by-step guide for how to get there, I couldn't envision myself at a new destination. After watching my school plans not work out, suffering a disappointing marriage, and moving ten times within four years, it felt like long-term plans for my life never worked out. Since I couldn't count on them, I stopped dreaming.

The morning when I sensed God say, *The only person keeping you stuck is yourself*, the morning I accepted the dare, I didn't feel courageous. I had a vague picture of myself speaking to a group of a hundred people, and I noticed a desire to write that never went away. With no dream, no plan, and fear keeping me hostage, I needed to practice courage. So, I decided that for a year I would say yes to any opportunity that scared me. They weren't extravagant steps. I started speaking up in staff meetings, despite a red face and the risk of being misunderstood. I said yes to giving software training in leadership meetings at my church. I wrote an article for a magazine and joined a writer's association. Suddenly, courage felt more like excitement as I opened up to new possibilities.

Practice Gratitude

It's interesting how you begin to see what you train your mind to look for. For years I didn't realize how stuck I was in the drudgery of life. As I practiced being thankful for things I took for granted, I began to see more good things in my life. For centuries the Bible has been telling us to be thankful in every situation. In the past decade, research studies have been proving it. No matter what mood we're in, what hardship we're facing, we see life differently when we find little things to be grateful for. In your new journey you're going to come across setbacks and surprises. Establishing a rhythm of gratitude could look like making a list of ten things you're grateful for every night. Some people list whatever comes to mind. Others use prompts from categories of their life, such as relationships, work, health, impact, and progress towards their dreams. The important thing is to begin.

Flow Zones

I've discovered two rhythms for making progress on a new path: flow zones and power sessions. If your momentum depends on planning, thinking deeply and completing tasks, then fitting them into the margins of your life will only get you so far. Every interruption will dull your creative edge. In fact, plenty of research now shows that after a disruption to your focus, it will take you an average of ten minutes to get your mind back on track. Merely the anticipation of an interruption is distracting to me. When you lose yourself in your work, it's called flow, or being in the zone. The revelations and results you experience in this flow state come from a place of inspired creativity, connectedness, and confidence. Carving out regular flow zones is essential to building momentum on your new path.

Power Sessions

Of course it's not always possible to set aside hours of uninterrupted time to work on your dream, and you have to fit it into the nooks and crannies of your life. My business coaches taught me to carve out time for power sessions when I was setting up my coaching presence online. Have a specific task list so you know what you're doing, then set the timer for an hour—or even thirty minutes—and start crushing your list. The thrill of getting something accomplished raises your spirits and infuses you with hope.

Learn Something New

It's never been easier to learn new things. Just put a shoutout on social media, and you'll learn what people recommend as the best pizza, school, or daycare in your area. Explore YouTube, blogs, Udemy, and Creative Live courses, and you can learn the best way to record a podcast, start a side hustle, write a book, run a marathon, or begin homesteading. Endless books offer wisdom on changing your habits, maximizing your productivity, and becoming a more effective leader. The things you can learn are countless. In fact, if you love learning, it could be a procrastination method. You are only truly learning something if you can implement it. So, when you sign up for a course, read a blog, or attend a workshop, make the most of your precious time and energy by applying what you learn right away.

Stay the Course, Trusting There's Abundance

It's easy to get sidetracked by all the methods others are using to build their momentum. It's possible to invest in what will help your best next step without getting caught up in appeals to urgency. If a sales page is doing its job well, it will convince you that you need to sign up for the training immediately, or you'll lose the opportunity forever. Much like you might have noticed in your crossroads process, urgency raises something to the top of your priority list. Often that's necessary for us to make things happen. But if you have already sorted out your priorities, you can trust your gut. Does the urgency create anxiety about missing out? Does it conflict with your priorities? Does it try to convince you, *This is the only way*? Let it go. Bookmark it, accept the business card, or add the course to your wish list if you want to remember it, but also trust that there's an abundance of guidance ready for you when you'll need it.

Recruit Dare to Decide Friends

Your purpose, your dream, is part of a bigger story. That means you aren't meant to figure it all out on your own. Whether fear sidelines you, failure surprises you, or questions stump you, you'll get farther ahead when someone's in your corner. Yes, there's a season to protect an idea and not share it with the world. But there's something to be said for being part of a productive team. When you know what to do but find yourself avoiding it, maybe it's time to find a Dare to Decide friend. They will draw out your potential by keeping you focused and accountable. When the dream is too big to do on your own and all the daily steps are distracting you from the action that will actually move you forward, it's time to recruit help and delegate. It can feel foreign and scary at each new stage, but when you find the zone where you can thrive in your strengths, you can soar.

Before you know it, you'll realize you have a new normal. These rhythms will carry you through the stretching season of your journey. One day you'll be celebrating a milestone of success: landing a new job, finishing a degree, publishing a book, securing a high-figure business contract. Someone will eagerly celebrate with you and make some comment about being an overnight success.

Maybe you'll laugh at the notion, and only you will know the anguish, faith, and discipline it took to get to this point.

But your success will equip and inspire them at their crossroads, making room for dreams they never thought possible.

Dare to Set Progressive Rhythms

Which rhythm will build the most momentum for you? How will you get it in motion?

30
FINAL THOUGHTS

*"You don't think your way into a new kind of living.
You live your way into a new kind of thinking."*

—Henry Nouwen

The novels I was so fascinated with writing years ago now sit in a box in my basement, musty and yellowing. When you're stuck at a crossroads, unable to see a different future and yet longing for more, you might feel like those abandoned stories. What were once hope and happiness are now mere memories—dreams hidden from sight, neglected, and unlived.

If I stayed focused only on the outcomes I wanted in my life, I would see that box of stories as a failure.

But seeing my life as a process of becoming, of living with purpose no matter what comes my way, that box means something different than failure. Inside that box is a world of potential. It one day might be brought to life by wisdom and experiences I never had when I first wrote them. This time capsule holds records of a writing critique group that expanded my mind and skill, that helped me discover the part of me that had been put in a corner. Binders with handwritten notes in the margins prove that others saw potential in my stories and delighted in their possibilities. Pages of revisions hold lessons of imagination, maturity, conflict, desire, and character development—both mine and my fictional friends'.

Like that box, your crossroads is a treasure box of stories you get to tell with your life.

Acknowledging who you were, you get to be the character that changes to meet not only the demands of reality but of your new destination. Your past stories don't need to have a say in who you'll be in the next adventure.

The progressive complications along your path aren't interruptions in your story. Rather, they serve as opportunities to expand your capacity.

Finding your compass to navigate your next adventure will bring peace as you simplify your priorities. Others don't get to dictate your story. And while you have your part in authoring your story, God is working in the background, doing His part. You and God get to do this together, and sharing the adventure is half the fun.

As you sort out your options, you'll find the courage to face the facts and your feelings. Clarity will emerge as you sift through what God and are others are saying—and what you want to do about that.

Finally, you'll come to the moment when your life will change. You'll decide. Not the waffling decisions you've made in the past. This time, with deep resolve you'll take your next steps. You might freak out, or you might feel inexplicable peace. You'll fall and fail. Not everyone will see it the way you do. Sometimes you'll feel like giving up; other times, you'll soar. But there's no going back.

You can't go back.

Even though the adventure has only begun, you're not the same person you were when you felt defeated in your crossroads. You see opportunities and challenges differently, so you react and plan differently.

You have hope.

You even have more patience and adaptability for the journey ahead.

As you live out your decision as best you can, scene by scene, you'll be living a story you're proud to tell. Others will take notice. I know that's not why you're doing this, but people will notice, and they'll be inspired to find clarity and courage to live their own story.

APPENDIX 1

Congratulations! You've invested in yourself and your future by reading this book.

Our website will give you plenty of additional tools for your Dare to Decide crossroads. Make sure to join our growing Dare Club online tribe (daretodecide.ca/dareclub). We'll save you a spot! It's a great way to stay connected, focused, and encouraged.

If you would like further support through making your crossroads decision, becoming the person your dream needs you to be, and implementing a plan toward your dream destination—I'm in! Consider me your Dare to Decide friend.

We have a range of experiences that are ideal for you and your situation. Ranging from workshops to mini course to full coaching programs, Dare to Decide experiences help activate the principles you've learned where you need them most.

With support and strategy, these experiences offer the space for you to discover your dreams and uncover what's been holding you back. Step by step, you'll create your decision framework, sketch your personal growth plan, and map your adventure.

In these one-of-a-kind experiences, I serve as your transformation guide and spend time personally coaching each participant. Together, we'll uncover your dream and your Dare to Decide path.

You—and your life—won't be the same after this!
Go on, then! Dare to live your adventure.

daretodecide.ca

ACKNOWLEDGMENTS

Pursing a dream and turning an idea into a book is as hard as it sounds. It's internally challenging and some days grueling, but it's most rewarding. The process has helped me become who my dream needs me to be, and it wouldn't have been possible without my Dare to Decide friends.

To James, who spent daddy mornings with Lexie nearly every Saturday so I could have uninterrupted time to write. Your support and encouragement has meant the world to me.

To Dad, Murray Sluys. Thank you for sharing your story with me, believing in me, and investing in me and my dream. I'm honoured to continue your legacy of deep faith, working and creating from your passion, even amid hard seasons.

To Mom, Judy Sluys. Your wisdom, support, and lessons on grammar and creative writing have shaped so much of who I am today. I'm ever grateful.

To my beta readers, Tammy Palumbo, Lynette Doerksen, Emily J. Watkins, and Janet Collins. When I felt disconnected with my manuscript, you waded through those murky first drafts to show me its potential and how it spoke to you. Your support kept me moving forward, and your feedback made the book better.

To Laura Zeitner, Veloie Mastrocola, Mom and The Guild. Thanks for making my words shine.

To Mark Collins, coach Luc Lombardi, and every staff member during my years at Central Community Church.

You've been my light givers, kindred spirits, mentors, listeners, guides, and investors. Without your comradery, trust, and authenticity, I wouldn't be who I am today.

To Kary Oberbrunner, the Igniting Souls Tribe, and Author Academy Elite. You showed me the way and gave me a path for believing in my dream when I needed practical steps and companionship to continue the journey.

NOTES

Introduction
[1] "Americans' Beliefs about the Nature of God." Pew Research Center's Religion & Public Life Project. Pew Research Centre, December 31, 2019. https://www.pewforum.org/2018/04/25/when-americans-say-they-believe-in-god-what-do-they-mean/. Accessed May 8, 2020.

Chapter 1
[2] Cloud, Henry. *Integrity: The Courage to Meet the Demands of Reality.* Harper Business, 2009. pg 24.

Chapter 2
[3] You can find out more about how Mercy Ships sails to impoverished nations to perform free surgeries and provide training at https://mercyships.ca/.

[4] After twelve years of service in Central America, the *Caribbean Mercy* was sold in 2006 for renovation. https://www.mercyships.org/who-we-are/our-ships/the-caribbean-mercy/, accessed October 14, 2019.

Chapter 3
[5] Joel Houston, Matt Crocker, Benjamin Hastings. As You Find Me (CMG Song# 205442). Copyright © 2019 Hillsong MP Songs (BMI) (adm. in the US and Canada

at CapitolCMGPublishing.com). All rights reserved. Used by permission

Chapter 4

[6] Miller, Donald. *A Million Miles in a Thousand Years: How I Learned to Live a Better Story.* Nelson Books, 2009, pg 48. Since this book has been published, Don has expanded his definition, which you can explore further at http://buildingastorybrand.com/episode-65/.

[7] *The Holiday.* DVD. Columbia Pictures (2006). Written and directed by Nancy Meyers (2006).

Chapter 5: Choose Your Character

[8] This quote by Andy Stanley is all over the web, but you can access the full teaching in the book *The Principle of the Path: How to Get from Where You Are to Where You Want to Be* (Thomas Nelson, 2011) or the Your Move podcast, April 20, 2019 episode https://yourmove.is/episode/principle-of-the-path/ , accessed Oct 14, 2019.

Chapter 6

[9] Thanks to Brené Brown, who inspired me down the gremlin path with her shame gremlins in *Daring Greatly: How the Courage to Be Vulnerable Transforms the Way We Live, Love, Parent, and Lead* (Avery, 2012), Ch 3.

[10] https://en.wikipedia.org/wiki/Gremlin, accessed Oct 14, 2019.

Chapter 7

[11] Covey, Stephen. *7 Habits of Highly Effective People*, Free Press, 2004.

[12] Caroline Williams Yoga. https://www.youtube.com/channel/UC0n6WQ3_PAePXz_IZzXZFGA, accessed October 14, 2019. When I wrote the first draft of this chapter,

Caroline had 16,000 subscribers to her YouTube channel. With every revised draft, her channel gained thousands of more subscribers.

13 Caroline Williams, online interview with the author, December 2018.

14 I used to feel conflicted in the controversy about yoga stretches and some Christian perspectives on it. Caroline's articles researching both yoga history, context, and biblical understanding was a valuable resource to me. https://www.carolinewilliamsyoga.com/yoga-christianity, accessed October 14, 2019.

15 Williams, Caroline. "Yoga Mat Collisions by Caroline Williams," Collide, https://wecollide.net/yoga-mat-collisions-caroline-williams/, accessed December 12, 2018.

16 Ibid.

17 Williams, interview.

18 Ibid.

19 Ibid.

20 Caroline Williams, Instagram post, September 5, 2016, https://www.instagram.com/p/BJ_fFVKjTMr/.

21 You can find out more about Caroline and the ways she leads others to meet Jesus on their mat at www.carolinewilliamsyoga.com/ and www.theyogaabbey.com/.

22 Williams, interview.

Chapter 8

23 You can find out more about Tony Stolzfus and his transformational coaching at http://www.meta-formation.com.

24 Stolzfus, Tony. *Questions for Jesus: Conversational Prayer Around Your Deepest Desires.* CreateSpace Independent Publishing Platform, 2013.

25 Stolzfus, Tony. *The Invitation: Transforming the Heart Through Desire Fulfilled.* CreateSpace Independent Publishing Platform, 2015.

Chapter 10

26   Frankl, Viktor E, *Man's Search for Meaning: An Introduction to Logotherapy*. Boston: Beacon Press, 2006.

27   Ibid.

Chapter 11

28   Thanks to Melissa Fisher, who inspired me with her blog post, "3 Life Lessons I Learned from a Little Plant." Woods and Wool, April 8, 2018. https://www.woodsandwool. com/3-life-lessons-i-learned-from-a-little-plant/. Accessed February 15, 2020.

Chapter 13

29   Brené Brown, *Braving the Wilderness: The Quest for True Belonging and the Courage to Stand Alone.* Reprint edition, Random House Trade, New York, NY. Paperbacks. Aug. 27, 2019.

Chapter 17

30   Tricia Goyer, *Balanced: Finding Center as a Work-at-Home Mom,* Kindle ebook, GoyerInk. December 2013.

Chapter 20

31   Gilbert, Elizabeth. *Big Magic: Creative Living Beyond Fear.* Hardcover. Random House Canada, September 2015. Pg 25-26.

Chapter 21

32   Dr. John Townsend put words to what I discovered in his book, *Leading from Your Gut: How You Can Succeed by Harnessing the Power of Your Values, Feelings, and Intuition.* Revised edition, Zondervan, 2018. Ch 6.

33   This list was inspired by Dr. John Townsend's teaching series called "Now What Do I Do?" based on his book *Now What Do I Do?* Zondervan Books, May 10, 2010. The

session was called "Feel What You Feel," Cloud-Townsend Resources – 2014. Also, I discovered a similar list in Tony Robbins' *Awaken the Giant Within.* Free Press, Nov 1, 1992.

34   Don Colbert, MD, *Deadly Emotions: Understand the Mind-Body-Spirit Connection That Can Heal.* 5th Printing edition, Thomas Nelson Inc, October 1, 2003.

Chapter 24:

35   To find out more about The Birkman Method, see https://birkman.com/the-birkman-method/.

36   Loss aversion —I read an in-depth explanation with examples of aversion of loss in chapter one by Brafman, Ori, and Rom Brafman. "Anatomy of an Accident." In *Sway: The Irresistible Pull of Irrational Behaviour.* New York City, NY: Crown Publishing Group, a division of Random House Inc., 2008.

37   Commitment and loss aversion are two powerful forces that affect our decision-making. I read in-depth studies and explanations in chapter two by Brafman, Ori, and Rom Brafman. "Swamp of Commitment." In *Sway: The Irresistible Pull of Irrational Behavior.* New York City, NY: Crown Publishing Group, a division of Random House Inc., 2008.

38   The authors Ori Brafman and Rom Brafman call this "value attribution" and explain it with studies and more examples in chapter three, "The Hobbit and the Missing Link." In *Sway: The Irresistible Pull of Irrational Behavior.* New York City, NY: Crown Publishing Group, a division of Random House Inc., 2008.

39   Violinist Joshua Bell —You can read more about this experiment in an article by Weingarten, Gene called "Pearls Before Breakfast: Can One of the Nation's Great Musicians Cut through the Fog of a D.C. Rush Hour?" Https://Washingtonpost.com. April 8, 2007.

https://www.washingtonpost.com/lifestyle/magazine/
pearls-before-breakfast-can-one-of-the-nations-great-
musicians-cut-through-the-fog-of-a-dc-rush-hour-
lets-find-out/2014/09/23/8a6d46da-4331-11e4-b47c-
f5889e061e5f_story.html.

40 A deeper explanation about diagnosis bias and the study about the economics class can be found in chapter four by Ori Brafman and Rom Brafman. "Michael Jordan and the First-Date Interview." In *Sway: The Irresistible Pull of Irrational Behavior*. New York City, NY: Crown Publishing Group, a division of Random House Inc., 2008.

41 The Economics class study was first recorded by Harold H. Kelley of the University of Michigan. He titled it "The Warm-Cold Variable in First Impression of Persons" and published in The Journal of Personality, Issue 18, No 4, (1950), 431-39.

Chapter 25

42 I've been deeply impacted by Allie Casazza's story about how decluttering her home healed her depression and set her up to use minimalism principles for the rest of her life. You can read more about it in her article called "MY STORY." Allie Casazza. Accessed November 9, 2019. http://alliecasazza.com/allie-story.

43 This study is referenced in many blogs and articles online, but the original study was done by Shai Danziger, Jonathan Levav, Liora Avnaim-Pesso. It was called "Extraneous factors in judicial decisions" and published in Proceedings of the National Academy of Sciences Apr 2011, 108 (17) 6889-6892; DOI: 10.1073/pnas.1018033108.

44 Miller, Dan. *48 Days to the Work You Love: Preparing for the New Normal*. B & H Books, 2015. Pg 57.

Chapter 26

45 Miller, Donald. *A Million Miles in a Thousand Years: What I Learned While Editing My Life*. Nashville, TN: Thomas Nelson, 2010.

46 Thanks to Kary Oberbrunner for calling my attention to this. I think I first heard it in video online and came across it later in the chapter "Step Eight: MAINTAIN Your Clarity" of his book *Day Job to Dream Job: Practical Steps for Turning Your Passion into a Full-Time Gig*. Grand Rapids, MI: Baker Books, 2014.

Chapter 27

47 Based on phone interview with Murray Sluys by the author, January 2015.

48 Ibid.

Chapter 28

49 Donna Jo Hewitt, in-person interviews with the author, October 2015 and January 12, 2019.

50 Ibid.

Chapter 29

51 This workshop was co-presented by the author and Donna Jo Hewitt at Refresh Women's Retreat, November 2015 in St. Catharines, Ontario, Canada.

52 Donna Jo Hewitt, live retreat, November 2015.

53 Rituals —in some circles, the word *ritual* has a negative religious connotation. Others cringe at words like routines, habits, or rituals because the thought of pre-established actions sounds like a cage to them. Thanks Michael Hyatt and Allie Casazza, who also inspired me with their morning rituals. See Michel Hyatt and Megan Hyatt Miller, hosts. "4 Rituals That Make You Super Productive" *Lead to Win* (podcast) posted August 7, 2018.

Accessed November 11, 2019, https://michaelhyatt.com/podcast-four-rituals/?transcript.

54 See Allie Casazza, "5 Steps for A Purposeful Morning Ritual." Posted January 8, 2018. Accessed November 11, 2019. https://alliecasazza.com/blog/5-steps-morning-ritual.

55 See Caroline Williams, "Prayerful Meditation Practice to Slow Down in Greece" Caroline Williams Yoga, posted October 24, 2018, accessed November 11, 2019. https://www.carolinewilliamsyoga.com/secondary-blog-page/greece-meditation-practice?fbclid=IwAR1feCL0q8QvGISyEiqqtSW-t5wDH3HjafMPkftdu1gQ4W11RdqDPBu-4Sw

56 See Allie Casazza, "5 Steps for A Purposeful Morning Ritual." Posted January 8, 2018. Accessed November 11, 2019. https://alliecasazza.com/blog/5-steps-morning-ritual.

ABOUT THE AUTHOR

Emily Grabatin infuses hope into dormant and God-called dreams. Through her coaching, writing, and leadership, she helps individuals recognize who they are, uncover what they want, and streamline their focus so they can flourish on their Dare to Decide path.

Emily struggled through perfectionism, low self-confidence, and analysis paralysis in her journey to finding a meaningful path for her life. Today, Emily invests her time helping individuals become who their dream needs them to be.

She and her husband James live with their daughter near Niagara Falls, Ontario. Together they enjoy mini family adventures, bunnies and lattes.

Connect with Emily at emilygrabatin.ca.

DISCUSSION GUIDE

A transformational book needs to be discussed and
digested, not merely read.
Interested in talking through *Dare to Decide* in your book
club or church small group?

Download the discussion guide at
daretodecide.ca/guide.

DARE TO DECIDE EXPERIENCES

The purpose is simple:
Dare to Decide experiences help you discover dreams inside of you and uncover what's been holding you back. Step by step, you'll create your decision framework, your personal growth plan, and map your adventure.

Find support and accountability becoming the person your dream needs you to be.
Dare to Decide experiences range from online editions to in-person workshops.
If you're interested in taking your next step, discover the ideal path for you.

Visit daretodecide.ca